Failing Forward

Ted Roberts

HARVEST HOUSE PUBLISHERS
Eugene, Oregon 97402

Except where otherwise indicated, all Scripture quotations in this book are taken from the New American Standard Bible, © The Lockman Foundation 1960, 1962, 1963, 1968, 1971, 1972, 1973, 1975, 1977. Used by permission.

FAILING FORWARD

Copyright © 1984 by Harvest House Publishers
Eugene, Oregon 97402

Library of Congress Catalog Card Number 84-081214
ISBN 0-89081-432-5

Printed in the United States of America.

*To Diane and the kids
who loved me through my
failure, foolishness, and flouderings
and helped me to not only believe in myself
but to see the great thing God was doing in me.*

Contents

PREFACE

As my eyes scanned across the room I noticed an older gentleman sitting in the last row. He immediately caught my attention because there was a gentleness about him, but as I looked closer I noticed a deep sadness in his eyes.

He was part of a group of men who had gathered in a mountain retreat in Central Washington. This group had asked me to come and share with them. As I spoke to the men I found my heart returning again and again to focus on the gentleman in the back row. I quietly prayed that the Lord would make an opportunity for the two of us to get together.

On the second day of the retreat, between the practical jokes, water fights, and volleyball game, we got together. As we sat and I listened, the gentleman poured out his life story. He had been a tailgunner in a B-17 during World War Two. He had actually managed to fly 25 missions over Germany and live to tell about it. (Very few men survived such an experience.) The war, however, had taken its toll. In the ensuing years he had turned to the bottle, dealing with his hurt, pain, and personal failure through alcohol. The escape to the bottle always leads to only one place—a box canyon of despair. In the years to follow he was to see his family, his life, and his self-respect destroyed under the relentless onslaught of his addiction. He was a shattered man.

He looked at me and said, "Can God use a failure?" I paused in my reply because the question had so touched my heart. "Can God use a failure?" I don't think He uses anything but failures! We have all fallen and come short of the glory of God.

I started to explain all this to my newfound friend, but instead I simply said, "The Lord shall make your latter days far greater than your former." We hugged, and as we looked at each other I sensed that Jesus had brought hope to another pilgrim who had stumbled along the way.

The tailgunner is not unique. Over the years of my pastoral experience I have noticed that struggling with personal failure is a challenge not only for myself but for nearly everyone else as well. We may not hide in a bottle. Our lives may look quite orderly from the outside. We may love Jesus. We may attempt to follow Him with all our heart, yet there is a struggle going on, and it is with the nemesis of failure. It may not be such a lifelong struggle as that of the tailgunner; it may be a period of time when the roof caves in and all is lost, or it may be a period of quiet desperation where there is the oppressive sense of personal worthlessness. Whatever the form, whatever the circumstances, we all face the adversary of failure at some point in our lives.

This book is dedicated to my fellow travelers in the Christian life, those who have to deal with the daily challenges of living in a world where the only unpardonable sin is to FAIL. This book is not a clinical analysis of the dynamics of dealing with failure; it is instead the life story of many ordinary people who have faced the challenge and won. They are not invincible paragons of virtue, but common people like you and I, with needs, hurts, and limitations. Some will come from the pages of Scripture and some from the pages of contemporary life, but they all faced the tough times of dealing with failure.

I have adjusted the contemporary stories with respect to names and intimate details so as to properly protect confidences. The real identification point, however, is not with others but ourselves, for in listening to others we discover ourselves. In walking through the lives of men and women of Scripture we see ourselves, and more, importantly, we catch a fresh vision of Christ. He is indeed the same yesterday, today, and forever (Hebrews 13:8).

He is always available to help the tailgunners, the housewives, the students, the frustrated fathers, the troubled teenagers— everyone who comes to Him. He is the One who turns our failures into foundations for growth and our mistakes into miracles. We all need a fresh vision of the loving Christ and His faithfulness to us. I know that His vision for us is that our latter days will be greater than our former.

Ted Roberts
Eugene, Oregon

Failing
Forward

1

Learning From Broken Bootstraps

I'm sure you've have had the experience—you're in a hurry, and in the midst of your rush you exert a concerted effort to get your shoes on rapidly, only to have the shoe-strings break in your hands. Frustrating, isn't it? But life is like that for many people: Their bootstraps of inner strength have broken in two. Yet they are faced with more than the task of finding a new pair of shoes. They can't simply reach over in the closet of life and grab another self; instead, they sit with the strings of their soul in pieces and simply don't have the energy to tie another repair knot in the situation. Besides, the last repair job didn't work and, in fact, their life is beginning to feel like one big knot anyway.

At some time in our lives we have all faced the agony of such a situation. The terror is when the break is so severe or so persistent that we lose hope. I have seen the faces of men and women through the years in the counseling office who indeed have lost hope. They simply can't respond to the standard admonitions such as "It will work out," "Hang in there," or the all-time favorite, "Just believe—have faith." In fact, such spiritual placebos only serve to increase their pain.

A bootstrap response is absurd in their situation. They can't reach down within themselves and be lifted out of the situation. "Grin and bear it" has become "gripe and share it." Life has changed from rejoicing to ruin.

The Cover-up of Failure

It is amazing how infrequently the problem of failure is directly addressed today. If the subject of failure is discussed at all, it tends to be either denied or overanalyzed. The "how-to" books of our success-conscious society tend to simply brush failure aside as an inconvenient interruption on the way up the corporate or spiritual ladder. The other approach attempts to probe the deep recesses of the human psyche in hopes of finding a hidden key which will unlock all the problems of the past. In the process, the individual is frequently lost in a sea of introspection.

But failure is to be neither denied nor overemphasized; instead, it must be faced and conquered. Our bootstraps may be broken. We may have run dry in our reservoir of hope, and faith may be only a memory of the past. But God has an answer. He has an approach to the problem which grips the reality of life with the hands of faith. HE TEACHES US TO FAIL FORWARD. HE INVITES US TO ENROLL IN THE SCHOOL OF HARD KNOCKS AND TO GRADUATE WITH HONORS.

The school of hard knocks is a required institution of learning in the course of life. The apostle Paul pointed out that we have all enrolled in this school whether we know it or not, "for all have sinned, and fall short of the glory of God" (Romans 3:23). It is the impact of our mistakes and sins, as well as the mistakes and sins of other people, which throw us into the agony of dealing with the failures of life.

Our coming to Christ at the point of salvation started a pilgrimage—the pilgrimage of wholeness. It is not so much a clawing struggle to the goal of health and wholeness as a process of experiencing health as we walk in step with Jesus. In the process we make mistakes. We sin even though all our sins have been forgiven in Him. We encounter the sins of other people, and sometimes we are simply impacted by the circumstances of life. All these factors, separately and in combination, face us under the generic title of *failure*.

The Qualified Teacher

Many people have presented themselves as teachers in the school of hard knocks, but only One source is truly qualified. Only in the biblical record do we find a clear textbook on how to graduate with honors. Only in the biblical record do we find an explanation of the curriculum from God's perspective. Only He knows the beginning from the end, for He is the One who made us. We may feel worthless, but the Word of God says that we are His creation. Despite our mistakes, sins, and failures, we are His workmanship, created for good works in Christ. Our Creator alone is qualified to be our Teacher.

The perspective of the Bible is amazingly practical. It doesn't present "ten steps" in dealing with failure in our lives. Instead, it presents the lives of real people.

We see in Peter the original two-geared Christian—full forward or full reverse.

We see a man by the name of Moses burying his attempts at deliverance in the sands of Egypt.

We see a Saul of Tarsus viciously killing people in the name of God.

We even see Christ's disciples deserting Him at the point of the cross.

The list seems endless—but this is the beauty of the biblical record, for here we find real, breathing, bleeding people who know the agony of defeat. We shall look at just three of these biblical examples: Samson, Gideon, and Hosea. We could select many others, but our purpose is not simply biblical analysis but insight into the process of conquering failure. These three men from the Old Testament, two judges and a prophet, uniquely comfort and encourage us in the challenge we all face in the conflicts of life.

We may lose faith, but Gideon gives us the strength to believe again despite the fact that we want to run.

We may lose hope, but Samson helps us to rise again despite the fact that we sit in the dungeon of our own mistakes and weaknesses.

We may lack the ability to love, but Hosea helps us to love again despite the fact that other people have deeply wounded us and even God seems to have failed us.

More Than Just Stories

We will look at more than just the biblical stories. Hopefully we will get to know the men themselves, and in the process understand ourselves more clearly also. You may ask, "What good is it to look at men who lived thousands of years ago? We live in a totally different world. Gideon faced camels; we face nuclear missiles. Samson struggled with Delilah; we face pornography."

Obviously times have changed, but the core of the problem remains the same—fallen man. Paul saw the correlation clearly in 1 Corinthians 10. Many theologians have pointed to Paul's statements in this passage concerning examples or "types" as a reference to the types of Christ found in the Old Testament. Yet it is interesting to note that Paul primarily points to the examples as illustrations not so much of the character of *Christ* but of *mankind.* "Now these things happened as examples for us, that we should not crave evil things, as they also craved. Now these things happened to them as an example, and they were written for our instruction, upon whom the ends of the ages have come. Therefore let him who thinks he stands take heed lest he fall" (1 Corinthians 10:6,11,12).

Paul was removed from the events of the Old Testament by hundreds of years, but as he looked at the text he saw not only the character of Christ but a clear picture of man. He saw the cycle of failure which has haunted man since the fall of Adam. Our goal in this book is not an allegorical investigation of the symbols of the Old Testament but an *observation of the lives of these men*: a look at the way they think, feel, and deal with the labors of life; how they hurt and why; how they manage to believe God when faith no longer feels good; above all, how they succeed in spite of overwhelming failure.

In the light of their lives we should see with new perspective the nature of man and of his mind, emotions, and motivations. We will be amazed at how much they begin to look a lot like the fellow next door. And if we are totally honest, we will acknowledge that their struggles are a mirror image of our own. They provide a backdrop, as it were, to our own personal drama.

The years may separate us historically from these men, but we all belong to the same elite society—the Royal Order of the Broken Bootstraps. So let's meet three very special men of God, and in the process hopefully see our situation from a whole new perspective.

2

The Great One
Who Failed

In Judges chapters 13-16 we encounter the life of Samson. It truly is an encounter. It seems the man has never heard of the word "moderation." Everything about him is extreme. It is as if the Spirit of the Lord has painted the man larger than life on the canvas of Scripture. He appears to be a cross between Mean Joe Green and Bozo the Clown. He smacks of Hollywood. Yet I think if we look closely at Samson, his impulsiveness and inclination for selfishness, we also see ourselves. That is why he disturbs us so. To be honest, I don't think I have ever heard a positive sermon concerning Samson. Yet there is something about him which deeply touches my heart.

As I glance across my desk, my eyes fall upon a picture of myself, showing me aging faster than I care to admit. I see a young man standing beside his fighter aircraft ready to defend America. I know it is not considered fashionable to be proud of such things today, yet I am. Maybe it is simply my military background coming out as I read the life of Samson that touches me. There is something of the "John Wayne" in us all, and my soul is stirred as I watch Samson take on the Philistines single-handedly.

Yet there is something much deeper in my love for Samson. I vehemently abhor war, especially in a thermonuclear age. My love for him is not rooted in a fellowship of warriors; it is instead an appreciation for one of the all-time great bootstrap-breakers. Few men in the Bible are better examples of blowing it. Samson clearly takes the cake in the field of failure. It is in his time of the dark night of the soul, in his time of total loss, that he touches my heart the deepest. But more importantly, it is in his time of death that I find myself standing up and cheering. I find my heart saying, "Great comeback Samson! You made it!" My heart is won by a man who would not quit when all hope was gone. Samson was a man who kept going despite the deep agonies of his own mistakes. He was a man whose life can teach us how to fail forward.

Unknown But Crucial

It is important that we understand the character of the book of Judges before we look at the life of Samson. Along with Leviticus and Chronicles, Judges is one of the least read and understood books of the Bible. The Christian community has generally focused on such Old Testament books as Joshua or Exodus or the Prophets. Even Numbers has received more attention.

For the average reader, the name Judges conjures up pictures of men walking around in long black robes with gavel in hand. Obviously this image is absurd, but we could easily come to some false conclusions apart from an understanding of the historical background of the book. Therefore, let us spend just a few moments in reviewing this unique period of time in the history of Israel.

The period of the Judges covers the span of time after the death of the great military leader Joshua; in fact, it covers approximately one-quarter of the total history of Israel which is presented in the Old Testament, a period of 340 years, to the rise of Saul as the first king of Israel. It is the period within Israel's history where they have settled in the land of God's promise. They have been freed from the lash of Pharaoh's whip in Egypt. The people have heard of the miracles of deliverance from their parents. They have conquered portions of the Promised Land, yet there still remain large segments of the country under the domination of the enemies of Israel. It is a time of great promise for the people of God—great promise for blessing or for disaster. Not unlike ourselves, the people's choice was repeatedly to follow the lifestyle of the world around them and disobey God.

Tension in the Nation

A tension exists throughout the book and begins to surface in chapter two. The author states, "Then the sons of Israel did evil in the sight of the Lord, and served the Baals." This becomes one of the two dominant themes in the book which are in constant tension with each other. It seems that the children of Israel never learn. The minute there is a leadership void—the death of Joshua, the elders, or a judge—the people return to an attitude of worshiping the things of the world around them. Many commentators find this response particularly repugnant, but I find it the standard operating procedure in the hearts of men. Apart from the grace of God actively at work in us, we tend to return to the things that trapped us in the past.

The Christian church was to languish for hundreds of years until God raised up a Luther to bring the Word of God back to the hearts of the common man. In the 1700s England, along with France, was on the verge of a violent social upheaval. Yet in the grace of God, John Wesley appeared on the scene in England and began to preach of scriptural holiness throughout the land. Not only were many people gloriously saved, but the church was restored to new life and activity. The ensuing revival carried to the hearts of the people a fresh spirit of moral concern which transformed the manners and literature of England. A new philanthropy touched the prisons, revolutionized the penal system, abolished the slave trade, and gave birth to public education. It transformed a nation.

There is a tension in Judges: first the sin of the people, and second the grace of God.

> The hand of the Lord was against them...as the Lord had spoken and as the Lord had sworn to them, so that they were severely distressed. Then the Lord raised up judges who delivered them from the hands of those who plundered them (Judges 2:15,16).

A Tension of Becoming

How then are we to apply the book of Judges to our life? What is to be our framework of perception? As Christians we also face a tension—the question of how to live out the fact of Christ's Lordship in the details of daily life.

Much is being taught today about who we are in Jesus Christ, and this is foundational to the Christian life. We need to see ourselves as being seated in heavenly places in Christ Jesus. We are the sons of the Most High God, and all the riches of glory are ours in Christ. This is the Promised Land of the church. It is the inheritance of the saints.

We as Christians live in a divine tension between the fact of who we are in Christ and the reality of how we are doing in the world right now. We may be in heavenly places but our feet are frequently stuck in the mud. I am always nervous with the individual who constantly lives in the heavens. It can become a subtle escape from the failures of the present. We are called instead to live in a delicious tension of *always becoming*.

Yes, I can do all things in Christ, but I need to face the fact that I just treated my wife unkindly. If I simply ignore the fact of my actions and point to the reality of the heavens, I live in a dream world of religion rather than in a dynamic relationship with Christ.

It is in the process of being *honest with myself* that the dynamic of the life of Christ is truly released through me. It is only in the disturbing challenge of facing my actions that I understand afresh my need for His grace. I need to recognize my failure, yet hold on to the fact of who I am in Him. It is a divine tension of supernatural growth into His image.

In the pages of the book of Judges we find Samson and Gideon, who faced the fact of their failures. They became deliverers of Israel despite their inadequacies. They worked out the fact of their inheritance in the struggles of daily life. They lived in the Promised Land but did more than just take up residence: They experienced a relationship with a God who was bigger than their failures, and felt the companionship of His presence in the midst of their failures.

Limitless Potential

Few men in life have had a greater beginning. Samson literally started life with a spiritual "silver spoon" in his mouth. The nation of Israel had been in bondage to the Philistines for over 40 years, and in the midst of that oppressive situation God acted. In Judges 13:2-24 we find the story of Samson's birth.

> And there was a certain man of Zorah, of the family of the Danites, whose name was Manoah, and his wife was barren and had borne no children. Then the angel of the Lord appeared to the woman and

said to her, "Behold now, you are barren and have borne no children, but you shall conceive and give birth to a son.

"Now therefore, be careful not to drink wine or strong drink, nor eat any unclean thing. For behold, you shall conceive and give birth to a son, and no razor shall come upon his head, for the boy shall be a Nazirite to God from the womb; and he shall begin to deliver Israel from the hands of the Philistines" (Judges 13:2-5).

Samson was called to be a Nazirite. The word comes from the Hebrew *nazir*, which means to be separate or set apart. In Numbers 6 we find the details of a Nazirite vow, but Samson's commission was unique: His vow was to be for a lifetime; in fact, it was to begin even in the womb. The Nazirite vow was normally for a limited period of time, but in Samson's case it was to be effective throughout his life. (Only one other individual in all of Scripture began his life with such a calling: John the Baptist.) By the very nature of God's commission and promise to Samson's mother we see the tremendous potential of the man. From the moment of conception, Samson was set apart to the purposes of God.

He was not only set apart to God, but God uniquely responded to him. After the initial appearance of the angel of the Lord, Manoah asked for a repeat performance because he had not been with his wife. Graciously the Lord responded to his request, and the angel of the Lord appeared again. After a repetition of the initial instructions by the angel, Manoah asked the angel of the Lord what his name was. The response of the angel of the Lord is most intriguing: "Why do you ask my name, seeing it is wonderful?" (Judges 13:18).

This dialogue sounds a bit strange to the Western ear, but to a Hebrew, a person's name was indicative of his character. Manoah wanted to know who the stranger was. The angel responded to the request for revelation by

using the same name which Isaiah was to use in his description of the coming Savior: "And His name will be called
Wonderful Counselor, Mighty God..." (Isaiah 9:6). We are
not hearing simply a statement of the angel being extra-
ordinary, but One who in His very Person and Being is
wonder. He surpasses human reasoning, thought, and
power: He is God Himself.

The preincarnate Christ has come to announce the birth
of Samson. Manoah described the incident accurately when
he cried, "We have seen God!" (Judges 13:22). The angel
of the Lord has come to speak of grace to His covenant
people who have turned from Him. John the Baptist was
also born of a barren mother, yet his birth was simply an-
nounced by the angel Gabriel. Samson, however, was
brought into the world with an announcement from the
Son of God. Samson indeed began life with enormous
potential and blessing.

One doesn't have to look far to see the correlation for
the Christian. Peter calls us a peculiar people, a royal
priesthood (1 Peter 2:9). We all were born anew into
tremendous potential. We have the resources of heaven
at our aid. We can do all things through Christ who
strengthens us. He didn't just announce our birth; He shed
His very blood that it might take place.

The Investment of God

This investment of the Lord is understandable in some
sense when we perceive the task that faced Samson. The
silence of Scripture at times speaks as loudly as its explicit
statements. This is particularly true with respect to the life
of Samson. In all the previous incidents where God raised
up a deliverer for Israel, one who would drive the adversaries from the land, Israel called out to God from a repen-
tant heart.

This time there was no call for help from the people of
God. The Philistines were the adversaries and the only op-

remain unconquered during the period
of the major reasons for their success
was the fact that they frequently at-
...milate the nation of Israel rather than destroy
...litarily. The lack of a cry for help to God during
...e time of Samson is a clear indication that the nation had
become spiritually comatose.

But in the midst of Israel's danger God calls forth Samson: "He *shall begin* to deliver Israel from the hands of the Philistines" (Judges 13:5). The tense of release is not accidental. In the deliverances which have previously taken place in the book of Judges, the individual raised up served as a rallying point for the whole nation. Not so in the life of Samson. By the very nature of his situation, he is called by God to fight alone. He is a unique illustration of God's grace to His people. Even when they have not called, He has answered. Samson is to awaken Israel. He is to defend a people who no longer know the difference between good and evil, a people who are little different from the world around them. It indeed is a difficult task. Realizing this fact helps us to understand, though not condone, some of Samson's erratic actions. He is a supreme example of the grace of God.

The last verse of Judges 15 is of special importance in understanding Samson because it gives us the context to truly understand Samson's point of failure: "So he judged Israel twenty years in the days of the Philistines." For 20 years Samson judged Israel in peace and victory! He did not run from one illicit affair to another. He judged Israel for 20 years prior to his episode with Delilah. For 20 years he followed hard after God and led a people who had even turned him over to the enemy.

It is fascinating to see how one verse of Scripture can so change a common perception of an individual. Samson was not simply a wild-eyed brute. He did not ricochet from one Philistine woman to another. He served Israel as a judge faithfully for 20 years, but he was a man with a timebomb ticking off inside him.

From Potential to Ruin

In chapter 16 the timebomb explodes. It is as if we are seeing before our very eyes the total disintegration of a man of God. He literally falls apart. Yet the failure is not sudden, for the cancer of uncontrolled lust has resided within him through these many years. It has lain dormant within his soul, yet apparent to the Spirit of God who has rested upon him. Finally it flares to the surface with glaring ugliness, devouring and consuming the very abilities of Samson. He was a strong man, yet incredibly weak because he had never learned to control himself. He has perceived the Spirit of God only in terms of power and has never dealt with the matter of Spirit-led self-control.

Now we see the fatal issue which leads to his total failure.

> Now Samson went to Gaza and saw a harlot there, and went in to her. When it was told to the Gazites, saying, "Samson has come here," they surrounded the place and lay in wait for him all night at the gate of the city. And they kept silent all night, saying, "Let us wait until the morning light, then we will kill him" (Judges 16:1,2).

The Philistines are sensing the downfall of Samson. He has destroyed them for 20 years, yet they don't hesitate to wait in ambush for him. The enemy of his soul is closing in for the kill. There is the smell of spiritual death in the air.

Samson wakes up in the middle of the night and promptly responds by tearing off the gates of the city! Now this was no small feat. The gates of the walled cities in those days were enormous. They were frequently covered with metal to prevent them being set afire during a siege; each weighed several hundred pounds. The amazing fact is that obviously God's blessing of supernatural strength is still upon Samson in spite of his flagrant sin.

Samson wakes in the middle of the night, probably from a sense of conviction, however vague. In his frolic during the night there is no thought of leaving the party. He approaches the city gates and doesn't simply knock the doors down but uproots the gates and takes them all the way inland to Hebron. The action of tearing out the gates is a conscious response to his calling. The city gates were seen as a symbol of the city's power during this period of time. Samson is once again attacking the power of the Philistines with devastating force.

Send in Delilah

How do you beat such a man? Simple answer: "Send in a Delilah." In fact, you don't need to send her in— Samson will find her for you! "After this it came about that he loved a woman in the valley of Sorek, whose name was Delilah" (Judges 16:4).

Once again Samson is back in Philistine country. Gaza was one of the five principal cities of the Philistines, and the valley of Sorek was also within their sphere of influence. Samson is toying with temptation. We are not told what motivates his actions, but it is obvious that he has come to make love and not war. The calling of God has dissipated in the caress of Delilah.

Judges 16 gives us the lurid details of the fall of Samson. It is frightening reading as we watch Samson stagger forward to the cliff of his destruction. He appears to have totally lost his senses; it is impossible to exaggerate the stupidity of his actions.

I watched a cartoon of the life of Samson with my children, and Delilah was portrayed as a Mae West type of woman—the lady who says, "Come up and see me some time, big boy." I had to laugh at the portrayal, but the absurdity of the cartoon is mild compared to the ridiculousness of Samson's actions. Yet that is exactly what sin does to us: It makes foolishness the norm of human action.

The Ultimate Irony

Now the narrative comes to an excruciating climax:

> And she said, "The Philistines are upon you, Samson!" And he awoke from his sleep and said, "I will go out as at other times and shake myself free." *But he did not know that the Lord had departed from him* (Judges 16:20).

Sin is a mocker. It rises with its Halloween mask to jeer at the participant and collect its due. Samson had done what was right in his own eyes, and now the Philistines were going to gouge them out. He had refused to submit himself to discipline, and now he was to be brought under the involuntary discipline of a slave and prisoner.

The most expensive lessons ever learned are the consequences of sin. Samson had so invested in sin that he was no longer conscious of the presence of God. He became numb to the tender touch of the Lord. As he rose to go he didn't even know that the Lord had departed from him. There is a cause-and-effect relationship in the spiritual realm as well as in the physical: If we sow in the Spirit we shall reap in the Spirit, and if we sow in the flesh we end up with Delilahs for companions.

For the Christian this is a difficult concept to balance with the reality of God's grace. Recently a young lady came to my office in the midst of a deep turmoil over her struggle with sin. She had come from a deeply stained past and found herself sliding back into old associations. I assured her that, in light of her repentance, God's grace would not only cover her past but would enable her to conquer in the present and would keep her from falling in the future.

With poignant clarity she looked intently at me and said, "That sounds like cheap grace." By the tears streaming down her face, I could see that her response was not flippant or hostile but the heart cry of a woman seeking to make sense of her world, her life, and Christ. After pausing for a moment to let her work through the emotions of her intense statement, I pointed her to the thief that turned to Christ on the cross (Luke 23:42,43). In his confession of Christ as Savior, while hanging on a cross as a convicted criminal, we see that the forgiveness of God is based on His grace and not our merits.

Yet the young lady's statement also points to a fact which is infrequently balanced with the grace of God. That fact is the consequences of our sins upon us. As we walk in sin we forfeit something of critical importance: the manifest presence of God in our lives.

The thief did indeed go to be with Christ in paradise, but by his actions in this life he had forfeited the joy of walking with God on earth. God's primary goal in life is not to get us to heaven, but to get heaven in us. He desires for us to walk with Him and enjoy Him here and now—not simply some time in the hereafter.

A repentance of the heart and mind is needed. This young lady instinctively understood the true nature of repentance. She saw with incisive clarity that mere words could not help her, but only the power of God.

It is in the heart and mind that has chosen to agree with God that the power of the supernatural life of Christ is released in us. She left that office an unchained lady. God was no longer her adversary. She now saw the consequence of sin in her life and the abundant supply of God's grace to her in the midst of her sin.

Samson, however, returned to Gaza a chained man. The eyes which reveled in lust have now been gouged out. The arms which once rippled with indomitable muscular strength now hang shackled in bronze chains. The once-proud head hangs in glaring nakedness. The grim reaper of sin has come and cut down a man of

God. He had been a towering man, but now he stands as a towering example of the consequences of sin untouched by repentance.

From Ruin to Restoration

In Samson's life we see a man of tremendous potential; we also watch with deep agony the destruction of that potential. He is like an airplane which has pitched forward in a fatal nosedive. The aircraft dives earthward with ever-increasing velocity, ultimately hitting the ground before our eyes with a frightening roar. As the smoke and flames subside, we read, "However, the hair of his head began to grow again after it was shaved off" (Judges 16:22). I love God's "howevers": The Philistines have brought Samson under submission and have stripped him of any strength; *however*, all these actions are emphatically reversed by the fact of Samson's hair growing again.

This verse is not just a statement of a physical fact; it speaks of a gracious move by God. There was no magic in Samson's hair; it was instead a physical statement of a spiritual reality: It expressed the Nazirite vow between God and Samson. In the sensual clutches of Delilah he had chosen to discard that Nazirite relationship. In the hellish despair of the Philistine dungeon he returned to God. Time and again I have seen men finally turn to Christ after their comfortable life fell apart. They had for years proceeded forward, oblivious of the impending disaster. They had ignored the warning signs of family disintegration. Their airplane of activities finally hit the ground, and in the tear-soaked reality of the morning after, they discovered the love of Christ within the dungeon of their pain. It is often within these dungeons of life that we discover the deepest lessons of life.

Verse 22 speaks of one of the deepest of those dungeons of pain—the pain of a man or woman who has fallen into immorality. I personally do not think there is a more debilitating sin. It is debilitating not because it deals with human sexuality or because God is a prude, but because it requires such a lifestyle of deception to walk in a pattern of immorality—a deception with respect to God, people you are influencing, and especially yourself. The reaction of the church today to the question of immorality seems to alternate between two extremes. The first extreme is to ignore the problem and hope it will go away. This approach may appear initially successful. The individual involved is usually sorry. Things can be patched up, and life can go on as before. There is, however, a ticking timebomb in the situation because the significant failures of life are not the product of a mere casual or flippant action. It may take 20 years, but failure untouched by repentance will erupt again in a more malignant form.

Burning at the Stake?

The other option is to burn the individual at the stake. This is a fear reaction. It is an attempt to quarantine by killing. This type of response usually looks at Samson as the classic example of a loser. He is unworthy of God's grace and in his sin forfeited his ministry. But I remind you of that beautiful passage, Hebrews 11:32: "And what more shall I say? For time will fail me if I tell of Gideon, Barak, Samson, Jephthah, of David and Samuel and the prophets." Hebrews 11 is commonly referred to as the "faith hall of fame." In chronological order the author lists some of the heroes of the faith. He refers to Abraham, Moses, David, and, of all people, Samson! God's view of Samson is that he is a winner despite his catastrophic failure. This is a summary statement of Samson's life, and God sees Samson as a finisher in the faith.

Samson is not alone in Hebrews 11. In fact, I would rename the chapter and call it "God's hall of reclaimed failures." For example, Abraham was frequently caught in the act of lying with respect to his wife. Jacob was one of the most deceptive men in the Bible. Moses started his ministry by killing a man and trying to hide the fact. David broke almost every law God ever gave. Rahab was a harlot. The list goes on and on.

Learning to Fail Forward

I'm so thankful that God doesn't respond to our failures as men do. Those around us tend to reject or ignore us in the midst of failures. But no matter how far we fall, it is never beyond God's forgiveness. Few have fallen as far as Samson, yet he was never beyond the restoring love of God. Our view of success is so easily tainted by the world's view, but we must understand that the successful Christian is not a failure-proof person. He has instead learned to accept God's remedy for failure. HE HAS LEARNED TO FAIL FORWARD.

In the gloom of Samson's confinement, he reached out and agreed with God. He realized that his uncontrolled behavior had finally caught up with him, but, more importantly, he discovered the forgiveness of God. To fail forward one needs to honestly accept responsibility for his actions. In Samson's prayer at the end of his life we see that he has faced that issue.

When we run from our failures, we end up falling backward, not forward. There is no progress in the pain. We go from one painful situation to another, never realizing our contribution to the problem. We may even be physically restrained, as Samson was in some sense, yet in our head we are still running. We and we alone decide when the running is to stop. If we never accept responsibility for our problems, then we find it difficult to turn to God for forgiveness. It is always someone else's fault. Delilah is seen as the reason I am stuck in this situation, or my wife, or husband, or boss, or parents. The list can be endless, but the list is the primary reason why the love of God seems so distant in the midst of the pain.

Samson dropped the list and grasped the forgiveness of God. It is important that we notice that the hair grew back but his eyes remained blinded. The Lord's purpose is not simply to forgive our past but to guarantee our future, and that kind of restoration TAKES TIME. It takes time because catastrophic failures are not a product of the moment.

But the story doesn't stop with Samson sitting in a dungeon crying out to God. It ends with him rising to his feet and accomplishing the task of his calling. Failing forward is also realizing that God is not intimidated by our failures. This sounds silly when we say it, yet many of us live our lives as if it were true. Severe failure in a person's life tends to make him introverted and defensive. He believes that God can love others, but after what *he* has done, God obviously views him as a second-class citizen.

The Restoring Love of God

The love of God isn't based on our performance but upon His character. He is faithful even when we are unfaithful. The mind and heart stagger at such love. It is a love which loves us in the midst of our failures, but even more it is a love which challenges us to yield up our failures to Him and recognize His lordship. It is in this yielding that we discover a motivation for life which is unstoppable, a motivation based upon the sovereign love of God. And so Samson takes the shattered remnants of his life and yields them to God. He cries out in the midst of the Philistines, "O Lord God, please remember me and please strengthen me just this time" (Judges 16:28).

He has been brought before the Philistines that they may "make sport" of him. I can see the scene vividly. He has been dragged out of the dungeon and brought before the Philistine festivities. He stands as a laughingstock. His garments are tattered; his eyes are empty sockets of scarred tissue; he smells of the dungeon, this fool of Philistia. They drag him before the drunken mob of revelers gathered to worship the pagan god Dagon. He is made to dance before them as a trained monkey on a leash. His fumbling jig at spearpoint brings taunts of "Behold the destroyer of our country!" from the assembled crowd.

He is then brought before the dignitaries of the Philistines and made to stand between the pillars of the building. This once-great warrior of Israel is led by a mere boy. He is but an emaciated shell of what he once was. To the human eye, he leans against the pillars of the building as a total failure.

To the human eye he is a wasted husk of a man, but to God he stands as a prodigal son freshly returned from the wasteland of his wanderings. He stands not as a bald buffoon, but as a Nazirite, a man committed to the purposes of God, freshly available for the anointing of God. Then above the din of the Philistine merriment we hear Samson cry out to God for strength. This is the first time in his life that we find him seeking God before he acts, and he addresses God with three different names in that short prayer. In the dungeon he has come to know his God. We hear a prayer which has been refined through the pain of personal failure, a prayer born out of a personal relationship to God, a prayer of great power because it is based on the character of God and yielded in total commitment to Him.

Then Samson shouts, "Let me die with the Philistines!" The Philistine rulers freeze in terror as they hear the groan of a roof collapsing over their heads. They turn in horror to behold a Samson once again transformed by the grace of God into a mighty adversary. Judges 16 closes with the fitting epitaph, "So the dead whom he killed at his death were more than those whom he killed in his life" (v. 30). Samson rose above the dungeon. He transcended the prison of his own mistakes. He was a victor in the toughest battle anyone can face—being a total failure in the eyes of other people.

Responding to the Love of God

I will call his name John, but he was a Samson. He was a Christian who was in a dungeon of personal failure. He was holding up his fist to me not as a point of hostility but of explanation. "These hands are powerful. When I start to work on the heavy bag, people stop and listen."

John had found his answer in boxing. It was a means of dealing with his personal failure. He was punching his way through life. But his life had come to an end because his wife was leaving him. In dealing with a deep sense of failure he had learned to face life with a clenched fist. He had learned to survive in the dungeon and punch back at the Philistines. Yet through the woundedness of his soul he had been blinded, and in the process he was hitting those near and dear to him.

There are moments in counseling which I am sure will stay with me all the days of my life. As I looked at John that day, I was to experience such a moment. We discussed many things in the course of our hour together, but most important of all we prayed together.

It was a simple prayer, but one from the heart of God. I hugged him and expressed the Father's love for him in prayer. It was a love which understood his struggle, a love which knew his failure. But above all it was a love which challenged him to rise up and grab the pillars of his problem.

I am happy to say that John responded to the love of the Father that day; the roof of his imprisonment broke open that day. He had attempted to follow Christ for years, but now he was experiencing the joy of seeing Christ come to him. That day was to start a challenging process of digging out of the rubble of his situation, with the realization that God was not *against* him but *for* him despite his obvious mistakes.

I was watching another potential candidate for the reclaimed hall of fame.

Points of Failure—and Conquest

Many of us have points of failure, points where we made grievous mistakes, points of deep personal pain to us. Our situation may not be as bad as that of my boxing friend, but the agony is just as deep. The Philistines may be subtle shadows in the recesses of our minds, taunting us as we attempt to respond to the call of God in our lives. I had such a private dungeon. I had been part of a church which was facing a critical financial decision. I was asked to help the business manager present his proposal to the congregation after the morning service. Little did I know that the finances of the church were in total disarray. In six short months the church was to literally fall apart, and I had been party to leading over 50 families of the church into a financial box canyon.

Words cannot describe the agony of my soul over the actions of that day. I was to spend many painful hours reviewing my gullibility and its impact on other people. In the ensuing months I was to learn for myself the necessity of failing forward. I invited the Spirit of God to search my heart and identify areas within my character which set me up for such gullibility. I realized also that God was not threatened by my failure. He had called me to minister to His people, and I needed to get on with the joy of serving Him. But there was still another element in the process of handling failure that I needed to learn: I had not died with the Philistines. I was among the living and had to understand the challenge of failure from the perspective of daily life.

The answer to my agony came one evening over a year after the financial crisis as I reviewed the victories of a recent ministry trip with my wife. I recounted with excitement what the Lord had accomplished in the week of ministry. She listened with great interest, then with a perceptivity seasoned by a heart uniquely attuned to the

Lord she said, "Do you realize that you were equipped for that week of ministry by your failure of the past?" She was right. The topics I had taught came directly out of my agony.

Could the Lord have instructed me another way? Yes, but that is not the question. The question is what we will do with the failures of our lives. Will we hide them or mine them? There may be a few people on this planet who have never made a significant mistake after conversion, but I doubt it. The lessons we learn through failure have value to other people as well as to ourselves, God is not only undisturbed by our failures but His love is so sovereign that as we yield our failures to Him, they become points of growth for us. They become, if yielded, points of unique power. Paul put it well when he said, "Power is perfected in weakness" (2 Corinthians 12:9). How do we fail forward? By realizing that God's grace not only covers our failures but transforms them into distinctive points of ministry.

3

Yield Your Emotions

Samson's final victory pivoted around two critical events. One event was the pulling down of the pillars. The other was an event not directly detailed in the narrative. It was not seen by human eye. It was a victory of the emotions.

The physical details of Samson's defeat were excruciatingly painful: the devastation of his eyes, the physical abuse of imprisonment, the oppressive environment of his dungeon home. Yet these were minor compared to the emotional pressure of his failure—the agony of realizing that the Spirit of the Lord had departed from him, the echoing voices within his mind of the Philistines as they rejoiced over his weakness, but above all the crushing realization that he was a total failure.

Personal Prisons

Failure ignored, however, carries a tremendous price tag.

The individual may be able to get through the physical agony of filing bankruptcy. The wife may be able, in a relatively short period of time, to get a home functioning after the divorce. The young lady may date soon after the abortion. But the emotional impact of the failure runs far deeper than the physical damage.

How often I have seen the consequences of repressed failure surface in marriage counseling. Marriage counseling is much more difficult than ever before because of the high percentage of individuals who come to a marriage with a divorce in their backgrounds. The epidemic of divorce has attacked the very soul of marriage. It is as if our society has created a false escape hatch in marital relationships where the title on the door is "Divorce: the easy way out." Yet the door is a mirage—it leads to loss, not an easy escape.

I have a great deal of compassion for those who have gone through such a tragedy. However, divorce is an example of failure and whenever we ignore failure the price tag quietly escalates. Because divorce is now so socially acceptable, we tend to ignore the problem by blaming the previous mate, the mate's relatives, lack of money, or simply pointing to the fact that everyone is getting a divorce nowadays. The list is endless, yet the dungeon remains.

There was a woman I will call Joan. She was at the end of her rope in her marriage. Her husband was totally intolerable to her, his every move seemingly calculated to cause her pain. He would not express love to her children from a previous marriage with Joan also finding his children too wild and disrespectful. Their home had become a war zone of bickering and accusation. Divorce, for the second time, seemed the only way out. Yet she was in a dilemma—Joan was six months pregnant.

I was listening to another precious sister caught in the subtle chains of unrecognized failure. In our time together, we reviewed the characteristics of her present husband.

She was amazed to discover that she was facing the same problems she had faced in her first marriage, just in a different package. Her use of the pronouns "my children" and "his children" was indicative of a common reaction to divorce. It clearly pointed to the fact that out of the pain of the first marriage and divorce she had built her life around her children instead of her husband. But any marriage built around the children instead of the husband-wife relationship is doomed to failure. Our love for our children must flow out of the priority of our love for our mate. If this is not true, the children become "my pawns" in the power struggle between husband and wife.

Why had Joan built her life around her children? I asked her if their marriage had always been such a battleground. She responded with a gentle "no," and began to recount the beauty of their first days together. Why then had the relationship soured so quickly and deeply? There were many complicating reasons for the present condition but at the core lay one central problem: Joan had never dealt with the failure of her previous marriage. In the agony of the first marriage and divorce she had withdrawn into herself. In her struggle she had focused on her children. The pressures of her financial situation had also intensified her avoidance of the problem. In the disappointment of failure she had avoided dealing with its causes.

In the new marriage the old images had now come back to haunt her. The package was different but the problems were the same. Failure ignored soon repeats itself. Joan was being challenged that day to honestly face her emotions, the emotions which had motivated her to withdraw into herself after the first marriage. It had been a subtle process but the consequences were becoming painfully apparent.

It is in facing our emotions at the point of failure that we are challenged the deepest. They come as a swarm, replaying in vivid detail the particulars of personal tragedy, which intensify the very emotions of the struggle. It is a

vicious circle which places chains on our soul instead of
our hands, and physical release then becomes only another
form of bondage. The story of Samson is an example of
great faith, because few people make it to the place of pulling down the pillars. The reason is quite simple: They never
get out of jail. Like Joan, the dungeon of their failure quietly
haunts them, and the bars which keep them locked in their
personal prison are the recurring emotions they feel with
respect to the event. The event may have occurred years
in the past; it may not even be remembered on the plane
of conscious activity, but it has grown into a subtle plat-
form of perception.

Let the Stickers Speak

Joan's case is not unique because our society has taken
a twisted view of emotions. Recently I encountered a set
of bumper stickers which aptly expressed the problem. As
I drove home from work I saw the stickers which I think
capsulize the cry of our age: "If it feels good, DO IT" and
"Question Authority." Interestingly enough, these two
bumper stickers appeared on the same car. It was as if this
individual had attempted to synthesize the mindset of our
society. This four-wheeled philosopher was speaking his
mind on the state of the nation.

My mind raced back over the numerous counseling ap-
pointments I had been engaged in during the day, and time
after time the central issue had indeed been authority and
emotions. In our society we have developed a mindset of
questioning all external authority. In many ways I can
understand the forces which move people to such extremes. I will never forget the pain of listening for hours
to the grinding process of the Watergate trial. As if the Vietnam War weren't enough, we were now at war at home.
The very soul of America was being impaled. It was a
traumatic experience for the collective conscience of the
nation. Yet this is but a teardrop in a river of change among

the tide of human events within our land. Like the book of Judges, we have become a people where "every man does what is right in his own eyes."

The combination of the two stickers accurately points to the fact that we live in a society not only committed to the rejection of external authority but also committed to the authority of emotions. We as Christians would hopefully not expound our approach to life in the terminology of these two bumper stickers. Yet it is interesting how frequently we find ourselves thinking within the framework of the authority of emotions. Listen to the following comments and see if they sound familiar:

> "How can I possibly forgive that person after he has so abused me?"
>
> "How can I love my wife when I don't feel anything for her anymore?"
>
> "How can I trust God after this tragedy or loss?"
>
> "I feel like a hypocrite when I act contrary to how I feel."

Most of us have made or thought one or more of these statements at critical times in our lives. Though the situations may vary, the challenge is the same: How do we deal with our emotions in the midst of failure or extreme pressure? Repeatedly I have heard Christians state that they would feel like a hypocrite if they acted in opposition to their emotions in a certain situation. What they are expressing, though they may not know it, is the fact that their emotions are the critical factor in the decision process of their lives. But a hypocrite is not a person who acts counter to his *emotions*; he is a person who acts counter to his CONVICTIONS. A hypocrite is an individual who denies *himself*, and not simply his emotions.

A Crazy Society?

The question of emotions is uniquely critical for our

times. We live in an intensely stressful era. Otto Freidrich recently has pointed out that we have become a violently anxious nation. In his book titled *Going Crazy*[1] he has analyzed what Americans seem to do best and has come to the conclusion that it is "going crazy."

The famous Manhattan Study[2] came to the same conclusion. A group of distinguished social scientists investigated a random section of the city of Manhattan in an attempt to discern the degree of mental health present. Of the 1660 adults studied, only 18.5 percent were found to be free from psychiatric difficulties! The exact characteristics of the psychiatric symptoms varied greatly, but the vast majority of the difficulties were more than merely "mild." The conclusions are startling but undeniable: The majority of the inhabitants of America's largest city are psychiatrically ill to some degree.

When the combination of stressful society, supremacy of emotions, and wrenching personal failure is present, you have the potential of an escape-proof dungeon of the mind. Samson's victory was initially a triumph of the emotions: He faced and conquered the onslaught of emotions which naturally fell upon him in the midst of his failure. He was not controlled by the terror of his own sin and mistakes. The bars of emotional turmoil which formed the jail cell of failure were shattered in the moment of his repentance and personal accountability. But this moment of repentance and accountability can never occur with any finality if emotions serve as the presiding judge in the inner tribunal of the human psyche. The question of authority and emotions in the midst of failure is crucial. Apart from an outside authority, man is left either adrift in a sea of subjective rationalizations or in a dungeon of emotions over what could have been.

The Power of Emotions

Are emotions evil, or are they something we must deny

in order to face the personal challenge of failure? Of course not. If we look at the life of Christ, we find a full spectrum of human emotions. We read that He wept (John 11:35), wailed (Luke 19:41), sighed (Mark 10:14), and groaned (Mark 8:12). Even more important, we find that He looked on others with anger (Mark 3:5), spoke to some with indignation (Mark 10:14), and intensely warned others (Mark 3:12). He rejoiced greatly (Luke 10:21) and cried forth loudly in his soul-wrenching moment of desolation (Matthew 27:46). Jesus Christ expressed and experienced the full dimensions of human emotions. Emotions are not inherently evil; they are morally neutral. The question is what we will do with them. They can either support us or entrap us.

But what are emotions? Emotions, and in particular strong emotions, have been the subject of investigation throughout the literature of man. We find Oedipus gouging out his eyes, Hamlet killing his uncle the king, and J.R. being shot on "Dallas"—all episodes of the tangle of human emotions. Philosophers have attempted to understand them and psychologists have endeavored to analyze them. Yet until just recently objective evidence concerning the nature of emotions has been unavailable.

We know that certain types of drugs will produce specific emotional reactions. We also have come to understand that the lack of specific chemicals, such as lithium, can induce emotional reactions in individuals, and specific physical illness such as hypoglycemia can produce violent emotional swings in certain cases.

Yet behind all of this data lies the question of the relationship between the mind and the body in emotions. What are emotions? Are they simply a reaction to physical situations? The theory of Carl Lange and William James would seem to support such an assessment. Dr. James says that emotions occur because of certain stimuli. These are stimuli in the individual's environment which set off specific physiological changes. These changes trigger sensory nerves leading to the brain, which are then interpreted as a particular emotion.

What Makes You Jump?

I don't know about you, but snakes produce a strong emotional response within me. In my younger days I would occasionally encounter rattlesnakes, and the reaction was always the same: I would immediately jump straight up in the air with both arms and legs in rapid motion. I usually hit the ground about five or six feet from the initial point of contact and promptly exited the area. No words were uttered, no analysis necessary. It simply involved an explosive departure. Afterward, several miles from the scene of contact, I would realize that I was experiencing fear. Thus my response to snakes would seem to support the James-Lange theory.

But if the emotions we are experiencing are simply a matter of physiological feedback, we would expect that each major emotion would exhibit a specific pattern. If the mind is simply responding to sensory messages from our aroused bodies, then the arousal pattern must display a clear identity. Yet experimental evidence does not support such a supposition. No scientist has ever been able to find a specific physiological pattern for each of the hundred or so major emotions of the human condition. In fact it is very difficult to determine what emotion the person is experiencing simply by measuring physiological changes. Two individuals can report that they are experiencing very different emotions yet have exactly the same physiological states.[3]

Stanley Schacter of Columbia University conducted several experiments which displayed the truth that physiological labeling is not the primary process that occurs in human emotions. As usual, the participants were college students. Each college student was given an injection of the powerful stimulant adrenaline, and in sufficient amounts to cause significant emotional response. Then the student was placed in a waiting room with another student who was specifically instructed to act in a particular manner.

The requested manner of action was to be silly or giddy. Within a few minutes the student who had received the injection was joining in the frivolity. Another group of students was set up in the same way, but this time the student without the injection was instructed to act in a bitter, aggressive, and angry manner. The injected student displayed the parallel response of anger and hostility. In each case the injected student reflected the actions of the other student. The physiological effect of the adrenaline was the same within the injected student: The accompanying emotion depended upon what was occurring around him.

In a continuation of the experiment, another group of students was given the injection of adrenaline but this time they were specifically informed as to the nature of the injection and the physiological responses to expect. This group of students was much more resistant to the emotional influence of the other students encountered in the waiting room. They tended to emotionally isolate themselves from the other student. Schacter concluded from this experiment and several others that emotions depend on two factors: 1) physiological arousal, and 2) a mental process of interpreting or labeling one's own physiological sensations. The subjects who had received the injection but had not received any valid information about its physical effect interpreted their emotional state within the context of the waiting room. The other group understood the physiological signals of adrenaline and were more resistant to labeling their emotions in light of the other student.

Jukebox Reactions

Our emotions are an interesting combination of physical

and mental processes. An illustration might be helpful at this point in understanding the relationship. Emotional identification operates much like the old-time jukebox. The stimulus which triggers the emotional process within us is analogous to a coin dropped in a jukebox: It sets off the emotional process; the body is alerted for response. Sensory receptors in the body report these changes to the brain.

Yet the information is rather diffuse and general in character. The jukebox lights are on. The machine is poised for action, yet nothing can occur until the record to be played is identified. Until we punch the buttons to identify the record, the jukebox can't fully respond.

The human emotional process occurs in a similar manner. We are aroused by an external stimulus. The sensory receptors of the body inform the brain that such an arousal has occurred, and the brain labels the sensations. The labeling is generally done on the basis of either the environmental context and/or what we are thinking about at the time. By this I do not mean simply a spontaneous thinking; the labeling frequently can come from a rapid referral to past incidents.

Dr. Schacter's findings lead to a clear definition of emotions: AN EMOTION IS THE INTERPRETATION OF A CHANGE IN LEVEL AND QUALITY OF INTERNAL SENSATIONS IN A PARTICULAR CONTEXT.[4]

Emotions are the results of our understanding of our inner senses. Emotional feelings are the patterns of meaning we derive from within ourselves. We become aware of a change of our internal sensations and attempt to bring meaning to that change. We take into account our environment, our past experiences, and our overall perception of reality.

Once a decision has been made with respect to labeling, behavior will follow. In fact the labeling process tends to reinforce the bodily changes and intensify the feeling.

Rattlesnakes and Fighter Aircraft

Not too long ago I was ministering to a group of people in New Mexico. After the services I was taken to an outlying ranch where a young couple was attempting to build a Christian retreat center. They had literally carved the ranch out of the wilderness. As we sat in their small trailer, enjoying an evening meal together, I noticed a large rattlesnake skin pinned to the wall over my head. Avoiding the urge to rapidly leave the premises, I calmly asked about the skin. I was informed that the area was full of snakes at this time of year and that the one pinned over my head was killed just outside the trailer. I made a mental note of the fact and began to plan how I could jump from the front porch of the trailer into the truck on my return trip.

Still maintaining my composure, I asked how the colossal reptile had been killed. I envisioned high-powered rifles, hand grenades, or some other powerful weapon. With a sense of amusement my hosts simply responded by saying, "We cut their heads off with our shovels." They continued by pointing out that part of the process in clearing the land for a retreat center was to remove the snakes in the area. In fact the one over my head wasn't the biggest they had seen. In the ranch next door they had encountered a female rattlesnake over a foot longer!

Needless to say, my mind was reeling with the information they were giving me. A female rattlesnake! I had never stayed around long enough to figure out what sex they were. The buttons on my jukebox with respect to rattlesnakes were all prepunched, and the music wasn't a waltz! Yet my gracious hosts played an entirely different tune. They understood the nature of the rattlesnakes and were not intimidated by them. I don't think I have ever seen a clearer illustration of how perception determines emotions. Proverbs 23:7 sums up the facts nicely when it says, "As [a man] thinks within himself, so he is."

As we talked together that evening, some of my self-respect returned as I discovered that they struggled with flying. It was a challenge for them to board any aircraft, and to envision themselves twisting rapidly through the sky in an acrobatic aircraft was unthinkable. Yet this activity for me would be total joy. They worked in the middle of a wilderness area and routinely dealt with snakes. I had flown fighter aircraft for years and had frequently been involved in violent acrobatic maneuvers. Both activities involved danger, and I had seen a lot more people killed in aircraft than from snakebites. I began to see that statistically their fears were a lot more rational than mine. But more important, I could see in the contrast of our fears the nature of emotional labeling.

The change in level and quality of internal sensations which I had experienced in a rapidly maneuvering aircraft were labeled by my mind as enjoyment. The enjoyment was indeed stressful as I was alternately pulled up against the shoulder straps and compressed in the seat of the aircraft. Yet throughout these activities my mind was racing ahead to anticipate the next move of the aircraft.

Emotions are the spice of life. A life without emotions is like soda pop without carbonation. It would be flat and lifeless. Yet emotions wrongly handled can turn sour, and the wine of life can become bitter vinegar. It is in the midst of personal failure that the wine of life can become very bitter. The roar of our emotions begins to correlate with deep-seated patterns of insecurity which we all struggle with at times, and a vicious amplification of emotions takes place.

In the midst of failure it is difficult to deal with these emotions. In all failures we suffer loss: loss of prestige, loss of personal respect, loss of material items, etc. In that loss there is a natural grieving process, yet this grieving can become the foundation for a prison of the mind. We should not deny our emotions, as some would suggest. We need instead to honestly face the consequences of our actions and be open with respect to our emotions. Yet we cannot become *controlled* by our emotions.

"That's easy for you to say—you haven't been through what I have," might be a common response to what I have just stated. I have heard this retort many times in the privacy of the counseling office. It is a reply born in the agony of personal frustration, when emotions have become a deep enemy of the soul. Yet the circumstance of the personal situation is not the insurmountable difficulty; it is instead the *labeling process* which has gone on within the mind. The power of Christ is resident within us, yet too often we stay locked within our personal jail cell because we do not understand the power of our personal perception.

The Power of Perception

His name was Ehrich Weiss, and I have always been enthralled with his life and exploits. By his late thirties he had become the highest-paid entertainer of his day. You would probably remember him best by his stage name— Harry Houdini. He was the premier escape artist of his day, if not for all time. As is true of all great performers, his feats of escape were so unusual as to appear magical. Yet whenever he was interviewed by the press he clearly stated that his knowledge set him free. By this he meant that he spent hours upon hours studying locks, handcuffs, and other retention devices. He knew how they operated, and, more important, how to break them open. "My brain is the key that sets me free!" he often declared.

This strength of mind became an enemy one day as he faced a cell-door lock which he could not unlock. At the height of his fame, Houdini was challenged by a small town in the British Isles to try to escape from their jail. After much pomp and ceremony, Houdini was placed in the jail as everyone waited outside to see if he could once again escape from his imprisonment. For over two hours Houdini worked on the stubborn lock. Normally his nimble reflexes and rapid hand movements would unlock a door in three seconds flat. But this lock resisted all his energetic efforts. Finally in exhaustion he fell against the door. It swung open. It had never been locked! The only cell door which Houdini could not unlock was the one in his mind. His perception had so affected the facts that he had subtly transitioned to a jail cell of the mind.

In the pain of failure people also make such a transition. They look at the turmoil of their emotions and feelings and relate them to some tragic event in their lives. Initially our emotions are relevant to the grieving process, but soon they become bars which will not move despite all our efforts. Then there is a tremendous expenditure of energy as they try to rearrange the circumstances so as to deal with their emotions. This transition is extremely debilitating because it results in the construction of two false perceptions: 1) a focus upon the past—"if only," and 2) a focus upon circumstances as being the problem.

We could say that an individual taking such a view of his situation does not understand the ABCs of emotions.[5] He looks at the activating event in his life, which we could call "A." He looks at the emotional consequence of the event, which will call "C," and comes to the conclusion that after A comes C. But the truth of the matter is that A leads to B followed by C. The missing element in his analysis is B, his belief system. This truth can be seen throughout life. For example:

A (failure of an individual to notice you) equals C (I feel rejected and unimportant).

A (failure of my business) equals C (I feel worthless).

The difficulty in both situations is exactly the same: the belief system. In the first case the person being ignored *assumes* that the individual purposely ignored him. At a deeper level there may be a belief system that says he is being ignored because he is not worth noticing. The second incident assumes that personal worth is based on success in the business world. In both situations the *belief system* is producing the difficulty, and not just the event. A process of labeling has occurred which sets the stage for an endless sequence of personal recrimination and destructive emotions.

If this perception becomes fixed in the individual's mind, then the past becomes the stage of his life. The actors may be in the present, but the script is but a rehearsal of past events. The story is repeated again and again in the details of daily living, and the refrain of "if only" is constantly played as background music. The mental cell is complete and the bars of condemning emotions are in place. It is a self-constructed dungeon of the soul.

Tomorrow Is the Lord's

Samson was in such a position that he could not adjust the circumstances. But it was a blessing in disguise. He had to face squarely his foolish actions which delivered him into the hands of the Philistines. Then he had to correct the suffocating thought that because he had failed so miserably he was a failure. What a difficult task! He had to face the challenge of his emotions in the light of the overwhelming evidence which surrounded him. Yet he rose from the cell.

How did he accomplish such a task? How did he overcome the emotional load of such a failure? There can only be one answer—the love and forgiveness of God. He discovered that from God's perspective the door was open. At the moment of confession there was release. We so frequently attempt to pick the locks of our own prisons. We scheme and plan how we can compensate for our past failures, hoping for the big turnaround which will make up for past blunders. Yet life cannot be lived by waiting for the spiritual sweepstakes ticket. It is lived a day at a time. Yesterday is not mine. All its cares, pains, mistakes, and blunders have passed from my hands. It *was* mine, but now it belongs to God. If I attempt to change yesterday,

I am unable to respond to today. I become a reactor rather than a responder. I view all of life from the perspective of past failures.

Tomorrow is also the Lord's. It will be mine, but I can only meet it with peace as I live in the present. Those trapped in the jail cells of their emotions sometimes try to escape to the future. Yet that is merely a subtle form of avoiding the past. They are looking for the future to erase the past and make the present tolerable. They sit in the cell with eyes wistfully looking to the future. There is no attempt to deal with the lock on the door. They remain caged because they have not leaned against the present.

The Impact of Larry

There are people who will live with us forever— individuals who make a vivid impression on our very soul. Larry was such a man. I first met him in a seminary classroom. My first year in seminary was a severe trial, to say the least. I had stepped out of a fighter pilot's world into a strange atmosphere of Greek, Hebrew, and 15-syllable words. I had to carry a dictionary with me to even understand what these people were talking about!

In the midst of all of this the Lord placed me beside a very special man of God. The first time I noticed Larry was in the midst of a boring lecture. His feet began to bang uncontrollably on the footrests of his wheelchair, for he was paralyzed from a diving accident and had difficulty controlling his body at times. I appreciated the opportunity to wake up, but I was concerned for Larry. That incident soon became the foundation for a rich friendship between us. I became one of many people who gained a deep love for Larry. He was a man who loved life, a man who was living to his maximum in Jesus.

When our senior year came, the students voted upon which one of their fellow students they wanted to hear during graduation week. Well, you guessed it—Larry won hands down. I will never forget the moment. Larry wrapped one arm around the wheelchair, then leaned forward and stole our hearts. His ability to preach with such power was not based upon sympathy elicited from the listener. It was related to the wheelchair, but it came from Larry's response to the wheelchair, and not ours: He had decided to not let the wheelchair become a prison to him.

There are many stories of such courage, but Larry's spoke with unique poignancy to me. His condition was a result of a mistake in his life. He had jumped from a railroad trestle to avoid being seen, and in the process he had severed his spinal column. The tragedy had been a result of a personal transgression. It was an ideal situation for the construction of a jail cell of the mind. What a pity party Larry could have thrown! He chose instead to rise above his restriction and lean on the grace of God.

In the days and years we spent together, he was a constant source of encouragement to me. Frequently in school I would be facing a situation which produced great frustration in me. At those moments I would just look over at Larry, who was usually as disturbed as I, but on his face there would be an expression of determination. He would look at me and simply say, "Let's live this day for Jesus." He was a man who lived in the present and had also settled the issue of the future.

Obviously the pressing issue of the future for Larry was being healed. Healing is a difficult issue to approach with any calmness in the Christian community. It seems that positions have been taken and sides drawn, and the call of the day is to defend various theological distinctives. But I loved Larry's perspective: He would simply say that the issue of healing had been settled for him. He would lean forward with a twinkle in his eye and say, "One way or another when I enter the pearly gates I'm leaving this wheelchair behind." He had asked the Lord for health. He had settled the issue, and as far as he was concerned it was a matter of timing. He was contending for health and living in the present. In fact he was so free in the present that he would frequently pray for other people to be healed. He was a man not trapped by the past or future. He was alive to life *now*. He was a pursuer, not a prisoner.

Not Perfection But Persistence

Larry was an example to me not because he was so different from me but because we were so much alike. My points of failure may have not been so visible to other people, but they were no less real to me. In my past there were many wheelchairs. There were moments where I even looked more like Samson than Larry. In our lives the question can never be, "How do we avoid failure or painful mistakes?" We need to ask instead, "How should we respond to them?" Our mistakes and failures are only the evidence that we are human. The canvas of human existence is constantly dotted with such experiences, but we are left with the choice as to how we shall color them. Mistakes, failures, tragedies—they can become the dominant issues in a picture of morose shadows or the contrast points of an explosion of brilliant colors.

It is not easy to take a paintbrush in hand and begin to respond to the jail cell of failure with the brilliant colors of hope. Yet once we understand that in the forgiveness of Christ the door of our prison is unlocked, we can rise up and walk out free men and women. Our understanding and perception of His love transforms the terror of our emotions. Failure has no hold on us once we learn to FAIL FORWARD. The door swings open wide as we fall upon His grace.

When we speak of such a response of hope it is important that we do not understand it simply as an admonition to positive thinking. It is important that we learn to control our thoughts and approach the ordeals of life in a positive manner. Yet positive thinking alone will soon wither and die in the harsh realities of life apart from an understanding of the nature of God in the midst of our failures.

Losers Turned Winners

The Old Testament prophet Jonah is a classic example of how God deals with our failures. Jonah, as you remember, flees from the demands of God's love on his life and finds himself inside the belly of a large fish. After a period of swimming in the gastric juices of his problem, he is unceremoniously vomited on some beachfront property. Then the book of Jonah gives us a beautiful insight into the heart of God:

> Now the word of the Lord came to Jonah the SEC-OND TIME saying, "Arise, go to Nineveh the great city and proclaim to it the proclamation which I am going to tell you" (Jonah 3:1,2).

The implication of the verses is quite clear: *God is not intimidated by our failures.* He continues to speak to us right in the middle of our mistakes.

In the Gospel of Luke we find another Jonah of sorts. His name is Peter, and he is being churned in the belly of his own fears. Christ is arrested and Peter follows the soldiers at a distance. He hides in the courtyard, but, as is true of all Jonahs, the fish of his problem soon spits him out in front of everyone. Several people come to him and accuse him of being a follower of Christ. In total belligerency he denies that he even knows Christ. At this point Luke gives us a penetrating view of the heart of Christ:

> And the Lord turned and looked at Peter. And Peter remembered the word of the Lord, how He had told him, "Before a cock crows today, you will deny Me three times" (Luke 22:61).

The Lord turned and looked at Peter. What you see on the face of Christ in this incident is critical to your ability to face personal failure. In fact, what you think about God is the most important thing about *you.* A. W. Tozer put it well when he said that we tend by a secret law of the soul to move toward our mental image of God, and this is so true when we are under pressure.

Failure brings to surface our deepest concepts of God. The anguish of such moments can release a torrent of guilt and loneliness if we see Christ as our Accuser instead of our Savior. What then was the expression on the face of Christ? Paul gives us some very helpful information at this point. In 1 Corinthians 15, as he discusses the fact of Christ's resurrection, he mentions the fact that Jesus *first* appeared to Peter, *then* to the twelve. What a joy! It was as if Christ exploded from the grave to get to Peter.

I can picture the scene as Peter lies convulsing on the floor, sobbing with deep tears of grief over his denial of Christ. Then he hears a gentle voice calling to him. It is the Master. He has come to Peter. We don't know what was exchanged in the conversation. In fact, I doubt if Peter was able to say much, but I can hear Christ saying to Peter, "Remember, you are the rock." The first time they had met, Jesus looked at Peter and said, "You are Simon the son of John; you shall be called Peter" (John 1:42). Peter means rock. Jesus looked at this impulsive brute of a man and said that he would be a rock of stability. If ever there was a man in the biblical record who was not stable, it was Simon Peter. He spent most of his time exchanging his sandals in his mouth. He had only two gears, full forward and full reverse.

Peter was to follow Christ throughout His earthly ministry, but instead of getting more stable, he became less so. That is such a comfort to me at times—not a comfort to excuse my failures or to exonerate my sinful acts, but a touch of reality which allows me to be pleased with progress and stop punishing myself. The life of Peter helps us to see clearly that God is not intimidated by our failures. God in Christ never gives up on us. Thus we need to release the past, embrace the present, and leave the future to Him.

Peter did not remain an impulsive, unstable man. He was changed, but not by his own efforts. On the day of Pentecost he was to stand up and proclaim the truth of Christ. He was also the first man to take the news of Christ to the Gentiles. He became a rock in the church of Jesus Christ. But the transition came as he grew to understand the unconditional grace of God and the power of the Holy Spirit to transform his heart.

Yield Your Pain of the Past

There is another dimension of the grace of God which we need to see in the experience of failure: Our failures, mistakes, and pains of the past are odious to us. They carry the scent of death, yet yielded to the hand of God they actually become a unique tool in His hands.

I remember when I first entered the ministry. I was deeply troubled by the fact of my past family life. I had had seven stepfathers. Our home was in constant turmoil. How could I possibly counsel other people about having a Christian home?

Then I began to see the problem from God's perspective: He was calling me to yield my pain of the past. As I did so, I realized that I was uniquely equipped to minister on family life because I understood with deep appreciation the joy of a godly home. I began to see my times with my children in a new light. I could not only be the dad I never had, but I could also experience the joy of childhood which I never had. Flying a kite and playing in the mud took on new meaning. I had always wanted to do those things with a dad, and now I could. Out of the realization of the healing which was taking place in my life, my wife and I began to minister to others. We soon discovered that our experience was not unique. Many husbands and wives were coming out of a difficult past and were crying out for help. What I once viewed as failure in the past became a ministry in the present.

The specific nature of the failure isn't really important. It could be a tragic sin which you were involved in, an open rebellion against God, or even a failure of other people with respect to you. The question is what you will do with that failure. Samson repented in the agony of his cell. Jonah cried to God from the depths of the sea, and Peter went before the Lord. All these actions involve one thing: bringing the failure before the Lord. He and He alone can take what appears to be totally hopeless and turn it into an instrument of victory.

4

Healing of the Mind

The sun streamed in the window of my office as I sat listening to the young man. I was struck by the contrast of the light outside and the deep gloom which warred within this man. Jim was not an individual committed to the world; he had made a strong stand for the Person of Christ in his life. He was a loving husband and father, yet there was a constant struggle to experience the love of God within his own being.

We discussed the tangle of his emotions. I pointed out that his emotions were constantly leading him to wrong conclusions about himself and other people. He was frequently involved in a "branching" process in his emotions. He would experience a hurt or wound, which would lead to anger, which resulted in hostility. But hostility was infrequently directed against other people; it would focus instead on himself. His speech was constantly formed in a pattern of self-depreciation expressed in religious language.

59

He seemed unable to deal with his emotions and the stress of daily living in a redemptive manner. He was a man involved in spiritual vertigo, and the aircraft of his life was tumbling out of control.

Vertigo

The image of vertigo illustrates vividly Jim's situation. Vertigo is a technical term used to describe the disorientation that a pilot can go through at times in flight. In Jim's case of emotional vertigo he knew something was wrong but he was not even aware of the fact that he was constantly attacking himself. Life's daily failures simply became more bricks in the wall of evidence which entrapped him. The aircraft of his life was in desperate need of control, but his attempts at righting the situation seemed to only complicate matters further.

It is difficult to describe the experience of vertigo to someone who has never flown an aircraft under severe weather conditions. I can remember with intense clarity the times that I faced the challenge of vertigo while flying. It usually occurred during a time of stressful flying, such as attempting to land a fighter aircraft on a wet runway in the middle of the night. The difficulty was not so much landing the aircraft, though it might cause you a little consternation as the plane slides down a wet runway. The difficult part was getting the aircraft down through the clouds, ice, and rain so that you could land.

In the clouds my breathing rate would increase greatly. My flight gloves would become wet with perspiration and I would tense up in anticipation of facing some touch of vertigo. The challenge would frequently come in the middle of a turn. As the controller on the ground directed me to the airfield by radar, he would ask me to make various heading changes so as to avoid other aircraft and to be in a position for landing. The calm voice of the controller would tell me to turn to a certain heading. As I reached the desired direction and began to roll the aircraft out of the turn, another voice would enter my mind. It was the voice of my body. I had been in the turn for a period of time and my body had adjusted to the turn. When I rolled the wings level, my physical senses told me that I was in a turn in the opposite direction.

Fighting for Control

The phenomenon may be difficult to describe, but the experience is very uncomplicated. It simply boils down to this: Your feelings are screaming one thing and your mind is telling you something else. What makes the situation so tense is the fact that you are rapidly approaching the ground, which is very unforgiving to misdirected aircraft. How would I resolve the situation? I would focus on the instrument panel in front of me and ignore the flood of feelings which were screaming for attention. Actually it was not simple to ignore the intense signals of my feelings. In fact, at times the battle would be so severe that I would lean my body in the direction of the turn I was feeling even though I didn't move the aircraft. It was a classic lesson in faith. Flying by instruments in the midst of severe weather taught me, as few things ever have, to trust the facts despite my feelings.

But Jim's problem was more than a simple touch of spiritual vertigo. Like a fighter pilot, he was fighting for control. When he looked at the instrument panel of life, the signals he received were confusing. It was as if the instruments were giving him a mixed set of signals. Some instruments were telling him the plane was right side up; others were telling him he was upside down. No wonder he was struggling to know the love of God and his emotions were such a barrier.

Jim was suffering from faulty perceptions. His mind was misinterpreting his surroundings because of mistaken presuppositions. These mental patterns were releasing a

flood of emotions. He needed to be "rewired" in his thinking. Paul would have called Jim to be "transformed by the
renewing of your mind" (Romans 12:2). This is not a
simple process. It does not occur by just praying or by a
"confession of faith." It involves a total presenting of
yourself to God. As we have seen in the previous chapter,
our perception determines our emotions, and in Jim's case
false perceptions were constantly hindering him from conquering his emotions.

But why isn't it possible to just pray and expect the Lord
to transform our minds? Jim was a man after the heart of
God. Was there hidden sin in his life?

What Our Mind Is Like

How often I have heard men and women of God turn
on themselves with that kind of questioning! In fact those
same thoughts had already occurred to Jim. That was one
reason why he was at the point of despair. Since God is
not the problem, Jim concluded that he himself was the
problem. When you combine this type of thinking with personal failure, the results are devastating. This line of thinking
actually prepares the individual to fail, and once it occurs
the stage is set for further failure.

What is the difficulty? First of all, Jim did not understand
the nature of the human mind. For us to ask the Lord for
an instantaneous transformation of our entire mind is to
misunderstand the ministry of the Holy Spirit in our lives.
In Romans 8 Paul presents the vital ministry of the Holy
Spirit for the Christian. It is a ministry of relationship, a
relationship of freedom—freedom to walk in the love of
God and to enjoy life. In chapter 7 Paul was crying out
to God over the struggle of trying to live a life pleasing unto God: "The good that I wish, I do not do; but I practice
the very evil that I do not wish" (v. 19). In chapter 8 he
presents the solution, and it is important that we understand both elements of this answer. First of all, he points

out the fact that the Holy Spirit is our Enabler. He leads us as sons (Romans 8:14) and He helps us with our weakness (Romans 8:26). We cannot live the Christian life by trying harder. That approach to life only qualifies us for membership in the "white-knuckle club." You know the type—he is smiling at you, but every vein in his neck is showing as sweat drips down his forehead.

The Holy Spirit alone can empower us to live in the joy that God has planned for us. He and He alone can bring us to rest in the midst of a thermonuclear age. Yet chapter 8 also sets forth another participant in the process: "Those who are according to the flesh set their minds on the things of the flesh" (v. 5). Paul goes on to say that those of the Spirit set their minds on things of the Spirit. How we set our mind has a direct bearing on the effectiveness of the Spirit's ministry in our lives.

I emphasize this point because it is so frequently missed or misunderstood. Walking in the Spirit is not primarily a matter of our emotions; it is a thrilling response of the will to the initiatives of the Holy Spirit. Walking in the Spirit is ultimately defined by one word—obedience. This close dynamic of thought is seen by the wide range of meanings attached to the New Testament word for thinking (*phroneo*). The activity of the mind is not seen simply as an activity of the intellect but also involves a movement of the will. The biblical view of thinking involves both interest and decision at the same time.[6] It is a holistic view of the mental processes of man.

More Than a Computer

Modern neurological research has also given us a new appreciation for the importance of the human mind. It is important that we understand these discoveries so that we can come to a clearer comprehension of how our mind works in the pressures of life. The building blocks of the brain are the nerve cells called neurons. In our brain there exist about 100 billion of these living cells. This number has little meaning until you realize that it is about the number of stars in our galaxy.

But the picture is even more complex than that, because each neuron does not simply interact with just one other neuron. Neurons interact in a multiplicity of ways. In fact, the number of interconnections within the brain is estimated to be in the order of 10 to 800th power! As a point of comparison, this number is more than ten times the number of atoms in the entire *universe!* Truly our brain is a world unto itself.

The brain is also much more than a compact computer. Computers function by microscopic switches which can either be closed or open. In other words, they are somewhat like a series of light switches on the inside. The brain, however, does not function like that. The switching units in the brain (which are called synapses) can be partly open and partly closed. Instead of just communicating the fact they are open, they can say that they are four-tenths or nine-tenths open.

The switching units in the brain can also function both as a memory storage unit and processor at the same time. That is why we can be thinking about a problem and at the same time be in the process of remembering something out of our past. You are probably even thinking about several different things as you read this book.

The switching units of the brain also have the amazing ability to work with one another. They can respond to our surroundings as a network and retain a three-dimensional picture of an event, or even create an event through the process of imagination and association. We experience this as we dream. The brain is not only responding to its environment, it is interpreting it. The brain goes far beyond the most complex computer because it can take in multi-dimensional input, then transmit, store, and interpret the information along the billions of paths in the brain.[7]

If you find all of this rather confusing, suffice it to say

that the human brain is truly a miraculous creation!

The Marvel of Memory

Some people have responded to the previous information by saying that man's mind is nothing but a marvelous electrochemical machine. Obviously this position is in clear contradiction with biblical revelation. Man is far more than an evolving machine. He was created in the image of God. He bears the stamp of his Creator not only in the intricacies of his physical being but also in his spiritual nature.

Our memory is an intriguing phenomenon. I'm sure you have had the experience of your memory coming into sharp focus because of a distinctive smell, sight, or sound.

Recently I was walking through a shopping mall when the smell of Japanese cooking caught my attention. In an instant the odor triggered an entire sequence of memories. I recalled a moment while living in Japan of walking along the riverbank. It was during the time of a local festival, and along the waterfront many booths were set up to sell various kinds of foods. I remembered even the size, shape, and color of the river rocks beneath my feet. The memory was intense and vivid. Yet it was not from a time of stress or unique pressure. It simply was a memory which was stored deep within my mind.

Until recently such experiences were dismissed in scientific circles as purely anecdotal, but in 1961 a Canadian neurosurgeon by the name of Dr. Wilder Penfield changed our view of human memory. In Dr. Penfield's research concerning the nature of epilepsy, he uncovered some very significant facts with respect to the human mind. His work involved the stimulation of brain tissue of fully conscious patients through electrodes. His initial object was to identify the damaged area of the brain causing the epilepsy. An unexpected result of his research was the discovery that electrode stimulation of the patient would frequently result in the individual spontaneously remembering vivid events from his past.

Dr. Penfield relates one incident where the patient was recalling an incident on a farm with his cousins. The patient laughed as he relived the incident from the past yet at the very same time was astonished that he could be fully conscious of lying on an operating table in the present. Dr. Penfield commented, "The mind of the patient was as independent of the reflex action (the electrode) as was the mind of the surgeon who listened and strove to understand."[8]

In light of this evidence it is no longer valid to refer to the mind as only a computer. It is indeed a powerful computer, but there is more to man's mind than bytes. The computer of the human mind has a programmer, and he is using it as a tool of recall and motor coordination. Dr. Penfield summed it up well when he said, "If we liken the brain to a computer, man has a computer, not is a computer."[9] The mind has a computer, the brain, which man constantly programs to fit into his own world of varying goals and objectives.

Your Inner Heart

Where does biblical truth and daily living fit into all this? The Scriptures do not view man as a machine or as a collection of isolated parts. Various elements do exist within man, but the biblical viewpoint is one of unity. The unity of man is the underlying perspective of Scripture.

The Scriptures refer to the higher elements of man by such words as spirit, soul, heart, and mind, and to the lower elements by such terms as flesh, dust, bowels, and body. Yet throughout Scripture there is an implicit sense of the unity of man. He is not an electrochemical computer. He is not a spirit inhabiting a shell known as the body. (That is an early heresy which the church challenged and refuted.) We cannot classify every problem as being only spiritual. It is true that man's problems are *ultimately* spiritual, but in the living out of a life pleasing before the Lord it is critical that we understand the interrelatedness of man's being.

Of all the various terms which the Bible uses to describe man and the nature of his being, one stands out with particular importance: heart. The term is used over 800 times in the biblical text, and it especially illustrates man's unity or disunity as a complex body-mind-spirit-soul entity. The Bible's breadth of usage of the word "heart" indicates that it is clearly seen as something more than an organ for pumping blood.

Our English use of the word tends to emphasize the emotional aspects of the heart. My wife is preparing valentines for our children as I busily work at the typewriter, and on each of the valentines appears a large red heart. The heart is symbolized on the valentines as the seat of our emotions, and the Scriptures use similar symbology. The heart can love and hate. It can express joy or sorrow, despair and compassion.

> You shall not hate your fellow-countryman in your heart (Leviticus 19:17).

> And shout for joy, all you who are upright in heart (Psalm 32:11).

> Say to those with anxious heart, "Take courage, fear not" (Isaiah 35:4).

> . . . singing and making melody with your heart to the Lord (Ephesians 5:19).

Yet the common definition of heart as being the seat of our emotions is not nearly broad enough to encompass the biblical viewpoint. The heart of man is seen as also being directly connected with the thought-life of man.

> Then the Lord saw that the wickedness of man was great on the earth and that every intent of the thoughts of his heart was only evil continually (Genesis 6:5).

> Make your ear attentive to wisdom, incline your heart to understanding (Proverbs 2:2).

> Let the words of my mouth and the meditation of my heart be acceptable in Thy sight (Psalm 19:14).

> If you confess with your mouth Jesus as Lord, and believe in your heart that God raised Him from the dead, you shall be saved (Romans 10:9).

The Scriptures reveal that man's heart thinks, understands, meditates, and can be double-minded. There is a direct connection between the heart condition of a man and his thought-life. As we have previously seen, the thought process of an individual directly affects his emotional life, and his emotions reinforce his thought-life. The interconnection between emotions and thoughts is beautifully portrayed in the biblical term "heart." Yet the word carries an even greater depth of meaning within the biblical record. It can describe the moral character or volitional response of man.

> Beware, lest there is a base thought in your heart, saying, "The seventh year, the year of remission is near," and your eye is hostile toward your poor brother (Deuteronomy 15:9).

> Let your heart therefore be wholly devoted to the Lord our God, to walk in His statutes and to keep His commandments (1 Kings 8:61).

> . . . they show the work of the Law written in their hearts, their conscience bearing witness (Romans 2:15).

> Let us draw near with a sincere heart in full assurance of faith, having our hearts sprinkled clean from an evil conscience (Hebrews 10:22).

The heart of man is also seen as the seat or place of the conscience. It is the focal point of the will of man. It sits at the seat of the programmer. It gives direction to the computer known as the brain. That which comes from the heart of man is an expression of the whole of the inner man. It is a reflection of the inner convictions and attitudes of the programmer.

Yet there is even a deeper meaning of the biblical term "heart." It is also seen as the center of our spiritual life.

> When anyone hears the word of the kingdom, and does not understand it, the evil one comes and snatches away what has been sown in his heart (Matthew 13:19).

> But Peter said, "Ananias, why has Satan filled your heart to lie to the Holy Spirit?" (Acts 5:3).

> Because of your stubbornness and unrepentant heart you are storing up wrath for yourself in the day of wrath and revelation of the righteous judgment of God (Romans 2:5).

> . . . to be strengthened with power through His Spirit in the inner man; so that Christ may dwell in your hearts through faith (Ephesians 3:16,17).

The biblical concept of heart covers a diversity of physical, emotional, rational, and spiritual functions. It illustrates with dynamic clarity the fact that man is a complex unity of body-mind-soul-spirit. Heart is not simply an organ we can point to. It cannot be adequately symbolized on a valentine. It is not just the inner stirring of the spirit of man. It is instead an expression for the dynamic interrelationships of the spirit, mind, and emotions of man.

Tapes from the Past

Jim, the man who was tumbling out of control in his life, was under the false impression that coming to Christ results in instant and total transformation. He probably would not have expressed his thoughts in such radical terms, but he was treating himself as if it were true. There is no question that coming to Christ transforms the individual. The Scriptures clearly point to the transforming power of the love of God. But we must understand that the transformation is also a process. The apostle Paul put it well in 1 Thessalonians 5:23: "Now may the God of peace Himself sanctify you entirely; and may your spirit and soul and body be preserved complete, without blame at the coming of our Lord Jesus Christ." Paul is praying that the Christian's entire heart be brought under the lordship of Christ.

Man is more than spirit, and apart from an understanding of this truth we can find ourselves being deeply frustrated as we attempt to live the Christian life. Jim's problem had to do with faulty perceptional patterns. His instrument readings were constantly giving him false information. With our understanding of the nature of the human heart from a biblical perspective and the information concerning the neurological nature of the mind, we can see Jim's problem.

The heart or essence of man is found in the interrelationship of his spirit, soul, mind, and emotions. We are defining the soul of man as the interface between the spirit and mind of man. It involves the mind, intellect, and emotions. It is important that we not see the various elements of the heart of man as isolated parts but as a dynamic, integrated unity.

Jim was fighting with a cyclone of his emotions. They seemed to come in avalanches of oppression. He had prayed and sought God, yet the problem persisted. His spirit had truly come into a rich relationship with Christ. He had decided to stand against his emotions, and his desire was to follow the Lord. Why then was there such a turmoil?

This is a struggle which many Christians have faced. It is usually expressed by such questions as "Why doesn't Christianity work? I prayed and it doesn't help." Prayer is indeed the first step, but there also needs to be a REPROGRAMMING. In the experience of salvation our spirit is made alive to God. Frequently there is a feeling of a totally new beginning in life. Some old habits of the past completely disappear. I remember with great joy the experience of kneeling one night in Vietnam and accepting Christ as my Savior. After I returned to the United States I began to notice that I was radically different. For one thing I did not need to throw in swear words to punctuate my sentence structure. I had not tried to stop; it just happened. In the process of being born again certain habits of the past rapidly disappeared. Yet in many other areas of my life I realized that things had not changed.

I was still caught in the tyranny of habit. Certain attitudes and actions boiled up out of me with devastating results, and they became particularly painful now because of my newfound love for Christ. In the midst of these struggles I discovered the importance of Paul's admonitions to be "transformed by the renewing of the mind." It was in the thought process of my mind that the battle had to be won. Jim was also facing the same challenge. The thought patterns of his mind were giving him false indications with respect to himself, God, and other people.

The Lord will not magically remove these false patterns of perception. If He did we would be merely electrochemical robots. Salvation would be nothing more than sticking a new video cartridge in your head, and life would be very uncomplicated. But life is not simple, and we are called to walk with God—not be redeemed robots.

How Do You Perceive Things?

Over a number of years of counseling I have noticed that some patterns of perception run subtly yet deeply through the human mind. Some I would even call primal patterns. They seem to be part of the thinking process of most of us. "Primal" is a good term for illustrating the nature of the problem. According to the Scriptures, these patterns were there from the beginning. Genesis 3 presents us with the story of the fall of mankind. In verses 4 and 5 the serpent, as a spokesman of Satan, makes a paralyzing statement to the heart of man:

> You surely shall not die! For God knows that in the
> day you eat from it [the tree in the garden] your eyes
> will be opened, and you will be like God, knowing
> good from evil.

It is as if a poison arrow has impacted the mind of man. Instead of taking the accusation to the Lord, mankind listens, meditates upon, and buys into a false perception of reality. In the convoluted process of the dialogue with the serpent, the lie works ever deeper into the mind of mankind. Please notice that I said *mankind*. In verse 6 we see that Adam was standing there watching the whole process take place without saying a word. His was a dialogue of silence.

The destructiveness of the serpent's statement is not found in its information but in its implication. He is first of all implying that God cannot be trusted and that He is trying to keep good things from mankind. What a total lie! If you read Genesis 1 you find after each creative act of God the evaluation of "good." Then at the very pinnacle of creation the Lord makes man and woman and pronounces that everything is "very good" (Genesis 1:31). The stars are but stage lights for the love drama between man and God. The galaxies are mere background scenery for the expression of God's pleasure over mankind. God has brought to pass all of creation for man.

How subtly the world moved from creation to chaos with Satan's slur! If it had been a brazen lie I am sure it would have been refuted, but the sly accusation slid right through the portals of man's mind. Like an infecting virus, it soon infested the entire mental process of man, so that now it has become extremely difficult for us to believe that God is good and that He loves us. Our perception of God is deeply stained with negativeness. When we pray or sing "Lord, have Thine own way," there is normally a slight flinch because we believe that there is probably a lot of pain and agony ahead for us.

God Is For Us!

We can have many critics in life and survive nicely, but if there is a perception within our computer that *God* is against us, life becomes a ghastly inquisition. Our every move, act, and attitude becomes a stepping-stone to condemnation. We either constantly perform or we fall off the treadmill due to exhaustion and try to console ourselves with the idea that we are not as bad as some other people we know. Jim had such a God. He lived in the personal agony of performing for God. Instead of walking with Father God he constantly faced a divine foe. When you combine this perception with personal tragedy such as a business failure, a divorce, or the dumb things we all do, Christianity becomes a disguised form of agony.

In Luke 15 is a story which Jesus tells concerning the character of Father God. It is interesting that this story is normally referred to as the parable of the prodigal son. Actually it could more accurately be called the story of the caring Father. For one reason, it deals with two sons, not just one, and the focus of the story is the father, not the sons. One son left the household of his father and wasted all his inheritance. Yet he was lovingly and graciously received back by his father. The older brother remained faithfully at home and served his father, but never knew his love.

How much Jim was like the older brother! He was lacking the central element of the Christian faith—a knowledge of God's personal love for him. Like the older brother, he had worked, given, and literally slaved for the Father. At the core of his guidance system was the image of a demanding and powerful God. No wonder his instrument panel was a confusing jumble of indications! He would sing of the love of God on Sunday and would fight with a world arranged totally against him during the week. Life had become a divine obstacle course.

Jim's perception of God is not unique. I have begun to see that the major cause of emotional problems among Bible-believing Christians is the inability to comprehend, receive on a continuous basis, and live out in life the fact of God's unconditional love for us. That is a mouthful, but it is the truth. Why is it so difficult for us to understand that critical issue? The answer is found in the origin of the perception. As we have pointed out, it seems to be a primal twist of orientation within the "software" of our computer. It is only through the ongoing ministry of the Holy Spirit that we come to a proper understanding of God's love for us. Paul points out this ministry for us in Romans 8:26:

> The Spirit also helps our weakness; for we do not know how to pray as we should, but the Spirit Himself intercedes for us with groanings too deep for words.

The Spirit of God helps our weaknesses. Paul literally creates a word to describe the helping ministry of the Holy Spirit in this passage of Scripture. We translate the word simply as "help," but it carries a much richer meaning. It means to come alongside of and to carry instead of. What a beautiful picture of the ministry of the Spirit!

Moments of Healing

I remember well the first time I experienced this aspect of the Spirit's ministry to my mind. I was sitting on the floor resting against a wall of our bedroom. It was early in the morning and I did not have to be at work until late that afternoon. I had decided to spend time reading from the book of Romans. I was a new Christian and knew nothing of the Bible; as I read Paul's letter to the Romans I could not make heads or tails of it. My confusion only deepened as I read through the epistle, until I came to 8:14,15:

> For all who are being led by the Spirit of God, these
> are sons of God. For you have not received a spirit
> of slavery leading to fear again, but you have re-
> ceived a spirit of adoption as sons by which we cry
> out, "Abba! Father!"

I could read no further. I leaned my head back against
the wall and began to cry quietly. The emotions of anger,
hostility, and deep hurt which I had felt from my early years
began to just flow out of me. I began to see a loving heavenly Father at work in my life.

I had walked with my mother through six divorces. I
remembered the nights of hearing her head being slammed
against the wall in the room next to me, and the frustrations of facing an irate and irrational stepfather who had
an ability to inflict deep pain with his fists and deeper pain
with his words. I remember how in response to him and
others I had committed myself to never be intimidated
again. I had stayed true to that commitment: I became an
officer in the United States Marine Corps. I had developed
an ability to be tough if I needed to be. Yet as I read those
two verses of Scripture I could hear the Spirit of the Lord
gently yet firmly saying to me that I did not need to be
tough anymore. It was not a weak time, but rather a time
of great strength—the strength of the Father's love.

As I sat rejoicing over the Father's love for me, I began
to see a picture in my mind. It was a simple picture, yet
very powerful. I saw a giant pant leg filling the room.
Without hesitation I saw myself rising to my feet and running over and hugging that enormous leg. As I hugged
that leg in my mind, I could sense a breaking loose inside
me. I finally had a faithful Father—One I could look up
to, One who would not fail me, and above all One who
loved me!

Many years have passed since that moment of mental
healing for me, yet the moment is still fresh in my memory.
God had visited me that day. I had seen only one pant
leg (apparently in my mind God was too big to get both

legs in the house), but I knew that I was deeply loved. The Holy Spirit had been faithful to reveal the Father to me. He had met me at my deepest point of need. He had picked up and carried a burden that I had carried for years.

Moments of mental healing are intensely personal, because the Holy Spirit meets each one of us at the point of our unique need. He not only meets us there, but He communicates to us in terms that we can understand. Thus I would never make my experience a pattern for other people. We cannot make a principle out of our experiences; we need to let Christ be as original with other people as He was with us.

There is, however, a pressing need for the people of God to experience the love of the Father. It seems a particular problem for women who have been abused or sexually mistreated by a male authority figure. Their wound is deep within the computer, and they have learned to function despite the past pain. Their lives, however, lack luster; there is a lifelessness within their souls. Yet the Holy Spirit is faithful to meet their need as they release the past and call unto Him. Seldom is it as instantaneous as my experience; normally the revelation of His love comes over a period of time. The computer is slowly reprogrammed as they choose to agree with God throughout the process. Emotions may swirl about and pain from the past may resurface with intense force, but the Lord is faithful to walk with them and bring healing to their minds.

Biblical Positive Thinking

It is important that I make a disclaimer at this point. Some might read what I have just said and agree that positive thinking is important. I have not advocated a simple brand of positive thinking; I have instead contended for a biblical mode of thinking. God is love, a holy love. Before we were born He knew us and set His blessing upon us. This world is fallen, and in the midst of a fallen world we cannot miss pain, suffering, or tragedy. But despite all that, God is in control. He is not only in control, but He is *for* me, not *against* me. He can take the painful places of my life and turn the pain into a pearl of great price. He knows of the hours that I have stifled the tears, of the hurt that no bandage can heal. But, as Isaiah said of Christ, "Surely our griefs He Himself bore, and our sorrows He carried" (Isaiah 53:4). Christ not only knows of my sorrows because He is God, but He has experienced them as man.

It is on the cross that I see the answer to the patterns of my mind. I do not see a man being sacrificed to an angry God. I see instead God coming and dying for *me*. In light of that love I can yield the crippling patterns of the past. I can stand against the lie of Satan which says that God is against me. I can get off the performance treadmill and begin to respond to His love. I can hug Father God.

Breaking Free

I was speaking at a men's retreat not long ago and saw with my own eyes the stains of faultfinding within me, but also the liberating love of Christ. As I shared with the men I used a recent discussion with a new believer as a point of illustration. The young man had been hanging back in his walk with Christ. I confronted him and asked why he was so tentative. He responded by saying that he smoked, and so he could not be a first-class Christian. I told him that smoking will never keep him out of heaven, but that it will just get him there before me.

The men laughed at the story, but then I commented that I would like to take the rotten attitudes out of some "first-class" Christians and substitute a cigarette. It would be a liberating exchange.

I could not believe I had said such a thing! I had been raised in a strict environment once I came to Christ. I had just condoned what many of my teachers would have considered a sin! Well, as any speaker knows, when you make

a mistake just keep going. After the men's retreat, much
to my surprise, many men came up to me and said that
they had been set free from their cigarette habit. The desire
to constantly light up was gone. I asked each man what
had set them free. All the responses were exactly the same:
It was when I told the story about the new Christian who
smoked. They had subtly been categorized and trapped
by the opinions of other people as being second-class. Once
they realized that Christ did not view them that way, they
were finally free to deal with the habit.

Jesus stated the truth clearly in John 14:15: "If you love
Me, you will keep My commandments." For years I had
read that verse as a stern evaluation of whether or not I
love Christ. But if you look at the context of the passage,
it is quite clear that our Lord is speaking of *equipping*, not
evaluation. "If you love Me—if that is your basis of
motivation—then you will be able to keep My commandments." In the next verse He even adds the fact that He
will send the Holy Spirit, the Helper, to assist us.

Patterns of Grace

As I drove home from the men's retreat, I began to
understand some patterns that had been in my head for
years—patterns of rules rather than relationship, patterns
of grappling rather than grace. I found myself almost
fighting with those perceptional programs within my mind.
If I emphasize grace, then people will feel free to sin. We
dare not do that, since our society is already in enough
trouble. Then I remembered the charge against Paul in
Romans: "Are we to continue in sin that grace might increase?" (Romans 6:1). Paul faced the same charge when
he began to preach the good news of Jesus Christ. I was
finally coming to an understanding of the gospel, and it
marked a turning point in my life. I made a commitment
that day to speak of the reconciling love of Jesus, to emphasize His personal love to each listener—a love which

not only accepts us as we are but empowers us to be changed.

There are many patterns within our computer which cause us to constantly struggle with recurring battles and incidents of the past. Parents give us the data base for much of our perception of the world. An old Yiddish proverb underscores the importance of parental communication. "If one man call thee a donkey, pay him no mind. If thy father call thee a donkey, get thee a saddle." Emotionally crippled adults wear saddles today because sometime in the past they were called donkeys, not just casually but continuously. If you call your children donkeys often enough, they will line up to get saddled.

How do we deal with such debilitating patterns? Some would say that we need a "healing of the memories"—a cleansing or removal of those memories which cripple us. May I say as politely as possible that such a statement is absolute nonsense. Christ will never come in and wipe out our memory. If that is what you want, then pray for a STROKE. Our mind, we have seen, is a marvelous computer, and God desires for us to use it rather than remove it.

Try as we may, we cannot remove painful memories. We may repress or bury them, but we cannot erase them, for they have a nasty habit of resurfacing in other areas of our lives. They come out in the form of ulcers, headaches, and psychosomatic illnesses. The power of the mind turned against the body can be very destructive.

Deal with Your Memories

We are called instead to *deal with* those memories, to *face* those incidents of the past, and to TAKE RESPONSIBILITY for our reactions to them. If a parental figure has communicated rejection and lack of worth to us, we need to assert the truth of God's Word in that area of our life. The pain may still be present, but as we begin to view the in-

cident from God's perspective a unique thing takes place:
We gain perspective on the incident. It is no longer just
an experience of personal pain; we begin to see the pain
and tragedy in the individual's life who wounded us. As
we understand ourselves, we begin to see why others act
the way they do.

In accepting responsibility for our reaction, our mind is
no longer haunted by mental programs which trigger us
to despair and personal rejection. We gain an ability to face
the facts of life and not be intimidated by them. The process takes time because frequently we have said destructive things to ourselves for so long that we no longer hear
them. It will take some concerted efforts to ferret out the
false programs. We need to soak our minds in the Word
of God, especially the loving words of Christ. We may need
someone else to walk with us in this time of relearning,
someone who knows of the love of God. The emotions
will come and it will be easy to slip into the frustrations
of the past. But we must remember that we are never
defeated by anything until we accept in our mind the image of defeat. And Christ has settled the issue of defeat,
for we are overwhelming conquerors through Him who
loved us.

How is Jim doing? I am happy to say that he is becoming a fully certified instrument-rated saint. He may be a
little shaky in the clouds, but aren't we all?

5

Choose Your Reactions

Several chapters ago we began looking at the life of Samson. In the process we have discussed the nature of emotions and the neurological character of the mind, and have even attempted to present a synthesis of the biblical view of the inner nature of man. In the process of looking at Samson we have seen a reflection of ourselves.

Samson was not simply a man who lived thousands of years ago in a faraway land; his life transcends the years. It speaks to us down through the corridors of time. It speaks to us not so much out of uniqueness but out of his common experience with us.

It is true that his physical strength was a point of great novelty, but his appeal is found in the failures he faced— failures which are so much a part of daily living. It is in this area that we find ourselves standing with Samson and learning from him.

Emotions at Their Source

Samson conquered by first of all dealing with his emotions. How vicious our emotions can become as we hear the jeering sounds of our shattered dreams! Self-recrimination rises as a leering opponent out of the ashes of defeat. But Samson slew those adversaries with the only weapon that insures that they will not rise again—repentance.

Emotions are primarily a result of our patterns of perception; they come from the way we choose to view life. Repentance deals with the problem of emotions at their source. The word "repentance" is so frequently used in a religious context it is difficult for us to understand what it means.

I love to ask my children what various "church words" mean. It is an eye-opening experience. Time and again I find myself in the position of a pastor I recently heard about who called the children forward during the Sunday morning service. As they gathered about him, he started to give them an illustration from nature, but first he needed to ask a question.

His object was to have the children identify the physical characteristics of a squirrel, so he asked them, "What is gray, has a big fluffy tail, and eats nuts?"

Immediately a young man raised his hand in the midst of the group. The pastor then asked him to respond to his question. With a great deal of hesitation the boy responded by saying, "I know the answer is supposed to be Jesus, but it sure sounds like a gray squirrel to me."

I think children see the gray squirrels of life much clearer than adults; that is why I love to ask them definitions of biblical words. They have not developed a religious vocabulary and they are honest enough not to pretend that it all makes sense. They give us a marvelous mirror of common understandings of biblical terms.

When You Feel Sorry

Recently I asked one of my children what the word "repentance" meant. With the unadulterated honesty which only a child possesses, he responded by saying that it is when you feel sorry. His response summed up with vivid clarity the common view of repentance. It is a term little understood in the world today because people no longer have sins; they have "problems." They do not confess their sins; they "receive counseling." The unfortunate consequence of that viewpoint is that they do not experience a release from their struggles. Instead, they learn to cope with the pain.

It is understandable in some sense that biblical words are difficult to grasp at times. They are difficult not so much from the historical distance which separates the writer and reader; the struggle comes because Christianity revealed a new life and required a new vocabulary to express the new conditions. We can see this in the number of new words which appear in the New Testament. By new words I'm referring to Greek words and terms which the first believers devised for themselves. The actual terms may have appeared previously, but in their New Testament usage the vernacular speech was totally revolutionized.

The Changed Mind

The New Testament word which we translate as repentance is such a revolutionized word. The noun (*metanoia*) and the related verbs convey a deeper and more profound attitude of contrition than was ever known by pre-Christian writings. The pagan view of repentance was much like the popular view of today: It primarily meant to be sorry. The New Testament viewpoint is summarized by Paul in 2 Corinthians 7:9,10:

I now rejoice, not that you were made sorrowful, but

that you were made sorrowful to the point of repentance; for you were made sorrowful according to the will of God, in order that you might not suffer loss in anything through us. For the sorrow that is according to the will of God produces a repentance without regret, leading to salvation; but the sorrow of the world produces death.

The biblical perspective is one of a changed *mind*, not just changed emotions. Notice how Paul rejoices over the fact that the Corinthians have moved from sorrow to repentance. The Greek term literally means "a new mind." The secular meaning did carry a secondary sense of addressing the mind, but never to the extent and depth of the New Testament term.

Samson's response in the Old Testament is a picture of the New Testament revelation of repentance: He changed his mind. In the face of the consequences of his actions he chose to agree with God. To put it in Old Testament terminology, he turned to God.

Dynamic Transformation

There is a second element in the biblical concept of repentance which is totally foreign to secular thinking. In the process of being of another mind—agreeing with God—a transformation takes place. The sorrow becomes repentance by a response of our will, leading to repentance without regret and a deeper experience of salvation or wholeness in our lives. Repentance within a biblical understanding is not simply a response of man to his circumstances; it is also a response of a loving God to the cry of His people. There is a dynamic of God involved in the process; a transformation takes place in the believer as he faces the facts and agrees with God.

Oh how difficult it is for us to repent! We can find a million other responses or rationalizations. Yet it is only in the challenging moments of being honest with God that we see the chains of the enemy fall from our life.

Only in repentance comes a clarity of mind.

Only in repentance comes an understanding of our emotions.

Only in repentance do the chains of our mistakes, miscalculations, and failures loosen their grip.

Our families give us unique opportunities to experience repentance in details of our lives. We may never face a horde of physical adversaries in our life like Samson, or tear off the gates of our enemy's home, but we all face the daily challenges of being honest with ourselves, with God, and with those who live with us.

A Lap of Spilled Milk

As I sat down at the dinner table I had decided that I was going to be grouchy. I had experienced a terrible day. It seemed as if the circumstances of the day had stood in line to attack me. I had a right to be rotten when I got home, and I was committed to exercising that personal privilege. My response to the day was a clear illustration of how decisions lead to attitudes which result in emotional responses to other people, including destructive responses to the people we love.

One of the children reached for his glass of milk sitting on the table and promptly knocked it over. That was all I needed! I immediately launched into an oration about how there needed to be more order at the table. I did not yell, but it was clear to all that the master of the house had spoken.

Needless to say, my response was absurd. I knew it; even the dog knew it; in fact, he was so embarrassed by the whole scene that he got up and left the room. The kids knew it. They were trying to hold back the laughter. My wife was just looking the other way. She had taken a position of faith and was probably praying that I might be blessed with a swift correction.

But I was committed to be a grouch and I was determined to use my position as "head of the house" to justify my rotten attitude. Her prayer, however, was soon to be answered. After a few regal moments of silence, I reached for my own glass of milk and promptly KNOCKED IT OVER!

As the milk dripped down into my lap, I had two choices. I could ignore the raucous laughter of my family and desperately hang on to my pride and appalling attitude, or else repent. I chose to repent. Fortunately my family loves me so freely that they make it easy for me to repent. It is very difficult to retain a serious case of pompous pride in the face of such love. Wrong attitudes held onto in the face of correcting circumstances *soon become dispositions*. We lose the ability to truly decide, for our "decisions" become perceptional patterns within our computer, and destructive emotions become our comfortable bedfellows.

But failure and human foibles lose their sting when we choose to agree with the evidence that God has presented. When we agree with God a divine transformation takes place: We are able to break through the emotions and attitudes which have trapped us. We see ourselves clearly, and as we lift our hearts to Him who loves us and died for us, you and I see who we can be. In the light of His love for us our petty attitudes become intolerable.

For most of us the challenge is not found in a Philistine dungeon but in a lap full of spilled milk—in the daily decisions of life which either lay the bricks of our personal prison or the stepping-stones of our pilgrimage with Christ.

Repentance is a daily decision. We are being healed, in a sense, daily. The patterns of the past are being transformed as we walk in obedience to Him. Our emotions are being brought under His lordship as we undergo a daily renewing of our mind. We are becoming a people who set our minds on things of the Spirit, whether in a literal dungeon or at a dining room table.

The Challenge of Reactions

If walking in the Spirit simply consisted of a reprogramming of past perceptions and controlling our emotions in the midst of failure, life would be fairly easy. It is important that we understand the nature of our emotions and the character of our mind, but it is just as important that we learn to face the challenges from without. Sometimes emotions triggered from without can serve to erode the very health of our heart for God. Such emotions set us up to fail and to blame other people for the pain of our own actions.

Samson chose not to be imprisoned by his failure. He chose to break the chains of self-pity and personal regret and to turn the situation over to the Lord. As he faced the pressures of his own emotions he was able to grasp the pillars of his problems and destroy the enemies of his soul.

Some individuals, however, are never able to conquer the failures of their past. They can never make the first step in being set free from their turbulent emotions because their focus is misplaced. Their focus is always on someone else. For example, how far out of the jail cell of his mind would Samson have traveled if he had constantly blamed Delilah for his predicament? The answer is that he would have died there. The question may seem ridiculous, but it is amazing how frequently people project their guilt onto other people. The pain of the failure is so great that they cannot face their own responsibility in the incident. The failure of others is at times a difficult load to carry, but only we ourselves determine the ultimate outcome of our own lives.

In Christ, God has committed all the riches of heaven to us (Ephesians 1:3). He is able to bless us exceedingly abundantly beyond all that we ask or think (Ephesians 3:20). We have a sovereign, loving Father who is committed to bless us. He is actually working ahead of us, preparing in detail blessings for us. Situations in our life may not appear to be blessings at first glance, but God is always faithful despite our perception. Charles Swindoll put it well: "We are all faced with a series of great opportunities brilliantly disguised as impossible situations."[10] God in Christ has committed Himself to us. The issue is, Will we respond to His love despite how unlovely the circumstances appear? God has acted. The question is *whether* we will respond. And *how* we respond will determine our destiny.

You can see this battle in so many facets of life. The distraught wife or husband looks at you in the counseling office and says, "I cannot forgive my mate." Time after time I find myself saying with all the love I can muster, "Pardon me, but you used the wrong word. You said *I can't*; what you mean is *I will not*." The words may appear harsh, but sometimes the love of God is tender and tough at the same time.

We need to hear such a statement to help us realize that unforgiveness is a personal choice. Christ has settled the issue of our sins and has empowered us in the Holy Spirit to forgive the sins of others. Holding on to the Delilahs of the past turns us into spiritual convicts in the present. We can rehearse the failures of other people as reasons for our present predicament, but it will never free us from the situation; it will only lock us deeper into a cycle of failure.

Terminal Cancer

His name was Bill, and his face is still vividly portrayed in my mind. He was tall, thin, and ashen in complexion. I was soon to find out why his face was so gaunt and tense as he walked toward me. With little introduction or formality, he bluntly asked me to pray for him. Then he paused and stated that he had terminal cancer. The cancer was in the final stages of destroying his body, and he had only a few months to live.

I don't know how *you* respond to such situations, but I usually smile and go to full panic inside. I am really good at praying for headaches, sprained knees, the common cold, and other forms of "owies" my children bring to me. Terminal cancer is another thing. In such situations, however, the panic usually subsides and I have sense enough to come to Jesus. He and He alone can answer the terminal questions of life.

As I listened to Bill I was at the same time attempting to listen very closely to what the Holy Spirit might be saying to me. After we talked a short period of time concerning the exact nature of his difficulty, a unique thing happened. In the middle of our discussion I literally saw the parable of the unforgiving servant in Matthew 18 passing before my eyes. The implications were obvious: Bill's problem wasn't simply a cancerous rebellion of his body. Apparently this man was struggling with deep-seated hatred and bitterness.

I need to pause at this point. In no way do I mean to imply that cancer is always a result of unforgiveness or other negative attitudes. Nor do I believe that God can only heal through visions or other miraculous means. He uses doctors, medicine, prayer, miraculous interventions—in fact, an infinite variety of means. We can never forget that He is God and will use any means He sees fit to bring wholeness to us.

I began to question Bill about his feeling toward other people. I could see that the questions were irritating him. He wanted to be healed, not cross-examined. It soon became apparent to me that he was a very hostile man. Serious illness can produce hostility in individuals, but Bill's anger was much deeper than a reaction to a physical dilemma. He was bitterly angry at something or someone.

I continued to probe his emotions with little response until I mentioned the church. He immediately responded that he had always hated church, and in his retort there was an echo of deep rage. I asked him why he held such a view. He replied by saying, "I hate the church because my father was a pastor. He was nothing but a hypocrite." The word "hypocrite" literally dripped with hatred.

Forgive Without Limit

In Matthew 18:21 and following, Peter asked Christ how many times we should forgive someone. Peter thought he had an answer to the question and suggested that seven times would be a really spiritual response. Jesus replied by saying two things. First He suggested that 70 times 7 or 490 times would be a good number. Then He proceeded to relate a parable which pointed out that 490 times was only a beginning. I would love to have seen the look on Peter's face as Jesus responded to him!

The parable is actually a powerful three-act drama. In Act 1 we find a confrontation between a king and a servant who owes him around 6 million dollars. The servant cries out for mercy and says that he will repay the king. I'm sure the servant's response must have caused a chuckle from the disciples listening to Jesus tell the parable. I doubt that Peter would have laughed; he was probably still trying to recover from the 490 comment. The king, however, graciously forgives the servant and sends him on his way. This twist of the story must have brought forth a gasp of amazement from the listeners because such benevolence was unthinkable.

In Act 2 the plot thickens. The forgiven servant leaves the king's presence and proceeds to find another servant owing him only 16 dollars. He responds to the other servant by almost choking the life out of him and throwing him into jail until he repays the paltry debt.

Act 3 is the climax of the entire parable and is the specific answer to Peter's question. The king hears of the unforgiving servant's action toward his fellow slave. He responds not by throwing him into jail, but by handing him over to the torturers or tormentors. Then Jesus concludes the chilling scene by an even more startling statement:

> So shall My heavenly Father also do to you, if each of you does not forgive his brother from your heart (Matthew 18:35).

The Word of God is filled with promises. As I looked at Bill I was seeing a fulfillment of one of those promises. Here was a man who had been turned over to the torment of his own hatred. The torturers which Jesus referred to as a point of illustration were individuals who would inflict pain on a prisoner until a confession of his crime was made. It must have been awfully quiet after Jesus completed the parable. In fact, Matthew says that after Jesus had finished these words, He departed from Galilee.

Tasting the Bitter Fruit

God promises many blessings in Scripture, but we are also presented with our responsibilities. God loves us so much that He allows us to make our own decisions. We are not His puppets. The dark side of that blessing is the fact that we also experience the pain of our own destructive attitudes. One of the most frightening things that the Lord can do with us is to hand us over to our own destructive choices. He allows us to taste the bitter fruit of unforgiveness in our lives. He turns us over to the torment of our own unforgiving attitudes. Jesus is saying that we dare not keep track of the number of times we have forgiven someone. This attitude of record-keeping will eventually imprison us. We don't forgive someone because it is a nice thing to do, or because it is the expected thing. We forgive because God has forgiven us in Christ, and because unforgiveness is a deadly poison of the soul.

I asked Bill how long it had been since he had seen his father. He replied, "Ten years." My heart sank. He had placed his father in a prison of unforgiveness ten years earlier and had thrown away the key! Unforgiveness puts the other person in jail, and there is no way he can change. Unforgiveness chains us to the failures of our past. We may not see the failure as being our own, but as we hold onto it and rehearse the other person's sin in our memory, it becomes a personal point of failure for us.

As I listened to Bill describe his father, I heard in detail the final scene of the parable in Matthew 18. Bill's ashen face bore the stain of cancer, but at a deeper level it bore the lashmarks of his own unforgiveness. Finally I confronted Bill with his unforgiving attitude. I simply told him I could not pray for him until he chose to forgive his father. There were several moments of uncomfortable silence as Bill struggled with my comment. He responded by saying that he could not forgive his father. He was hurt too deeply.

Choose to Reprogram

Once we begin the constant rehearsal process of unforgiveness, it is very difficult for us to deal with our emotions. They become a consuming focus, and we associate forgiving someone with feeling good about them. Forgiveness then becomes an impossible emotional response.

Yet forgiveness actually begins with an act of the will, not simply the emotions. We must *choose* to reprogram the computer. Catherine Marshall put it well when she said that forgiveness is simply releasing another person from your personal judgment. It is not a demand to agree with the person or to even feel good about the individual. It is instead a refusal to assume the position of God. We must constantly remember that there are no nail scars on our hands. The unforgiving servant would never have imprisoned the other servant if he had simply remembered the debt that had been forgiven him.

So frequently we fall at the point of emotions with respect

to forgiveness. We may decide that we need to forgive someone, and then approach him about the matter. After getting through the discomfort of bringing up the subject, we work up enough courage to present the point of our struggle. The individual's response may range from astonishment to open irritation, but somehow we manage to discuss the incident without too much recrimination. Afterward we go our separate ways, yet there is this sense deep within us that forgiveness has not really taken place. This struggle is so common in marriages, and it sets up a merry-go-round of tangled emotions.

What we are really crying out for is a sense of harmony between us and the other person. Yet it will never come about by simply discussing our pain and listening to each other. That is the first step, but we also need to *act*. We must act in faith that the issue has been settled before God. In the process of acting we will fight through the fog of emotions which have been part of our previous thinking process. It is so easy to stumble at this point because our previous woundedness makes us hypersensitive to the other person.

Escaping the Combat Zone

In a marriage the other person can even breathe wrong if we are upset by some unkind actions on his or her part. The daily activities of life can be transformed into a combat zone of conflict. If this type of warfare continues over a sustained period of time, it literally begins to groove our thought processes in relationship to the other person. We don't have to figure out how we will relate to him. The standing battle plan is to attack and take no prisoners. The home may appear peaceful to the untrained observer, but the guerrilla armies of the couple's emotions are constantly at war. The lines have been drawn. She pours her life into the kids or her job. He is consumed by his job. Only barbed retorts of quiet frustration are exchanged.

Then comes a divine moment of reconciliation. It may have come in response to a sermon or to a time of personal Bible study or prayer. One or both of the parties sees the destructiveness of their relationship and their own part in the process. The couple is faced with a glorious opportunity to start afresh. Yet because of their previous hurts it is no easy task to trust again. They must climb up out of a deep habit pattern of thinking, and in the journey they will face the monsters of their previous emotions. Only the sword of concerted action in response to God's Word will slay those emotions and bring the couple into the intimacy they cry for. Learning to deal with bitterness and unforgiveness is a matter of life and death for all of us.

Two Kinds of Healing

Bill had been trapped into that deadly circle of equating feelings with forgiveness. It was literally killing him. I pointed out this fact to him. His response was guarded, but I could see that it was having an effect. It was like watching a great stone castle begin to fall apart from the inside out. I said nothing for several agonizing minutes as a virtual war raged within him. Finally he broke, and with a wrenching sense of relief he chose to pray for his father. There were no visible signs of any mighty move of God taking place— just a small group of men standing around a weeping brother who was coming out of a jail cell of unforgiveness. The tormentors were finally silenced. I and several other pastors then prayed for his healing. We hugged one another and went home. It was a supernaturally natural moment.

The following week Bill called me and said, "Ted, guess what! They took out the tumor and it was malignant, but they couldn't find any other traces of cancer in my body!" The doctors just several days before had said with total confidence that Bill's body was filled with cancer. Obviously they quickly adjusted their previous diagnosis to match the surgical evidence. A coincidence?? I don't think so. I have been ministering to people too long not to notice that when I stop praying and people stop forgiving one another those coincidences stop occurring.

How the Heroes Lived

We titled our chapter about the life of Samson "The Great One Who Failed." Maybe we should add a postscript to that title which says that God's great ones have also learned to live with the failure of other people. Abraham learned to live with the avarice and materialism of Lot. Lot always chose the best land for himself even if it eventually resulted in his destruction, yet even in the process of God's judgment of Lot we find Abraham interceding for him (Genesis 18). Throughout most of his life Abraham had to live with the mistakes of Lot.

Moses made many mistakes himself, but some of the most trying mistakes in his life came in dealing with his closest relatives, Aaron and Miriam. They not only attacked him personally because of his choice of a wife but they also questioned his relationship with God. Once a family fight starts, it seems that nothing is sacred. One can only imagine the pain within Moses' heart over the conflict. Yet we find him calling out to God on behalf of his brother and sister. Interestingly enough, Moses' only crippling failure came when he began to attack the people he was leading. In his anger over their unfaithfulness he assumed the position of God and was judged for his anger (Numbers 20:9-12). Bitterness and unforgiveness not only entrap us, but they bring a sense of folly to our lives.

God's great ones learned to live with the failure of circumstances as well as people. There is no doubt that people hurt us deeply, but circumstances can also ensnare us. Unforgiveness can take root in our heart over a negative event as well as a negative person.

I have always been intrigued and encouraged by the process in which Paul ended up in Philippi. In Acts 16 we find Paul starting out on his second missionary journey. He starts across Asia Minor (present-day Turkey) and attempts to minister to the various cities along the route. Much to his frustration and surprise he is literally hindered by the Holy Spirit from speaking a word in one city after another!

It is like watching a Ping-Pong ball bounce through the area. We could spiritualize the events and see some mystical manifestation of the Holy Spirit preventing Paul from ministering, but I am convinced that the Holy Spirit was speaking through daily frustrations. Paul got up in the morning and his donkey would not start! He missed travel connections. Once the donkey started, he broke down on the road. The list is endless, and after a period of time Paul began to sense that the incidents were not accidental but divine. God can lead by having our noses flattened against closed doors as well as He can lead by opening doors.

The important point is the fact that Paul did not stop; he kept going. He did not become hostile toward the circumstances. He would not allow a sense of woundedness to grow up in his heart. Finally, and I think with a sense of frustration, he rested in the little seaport of Troas. He had tried to be obedient to the Lord and had attempted to fulfill his calling as an apostle, but he had faced opposition at every point.

In the very midst of his frustration God spoke, sending Paul to Macedonia. I suspect that Paul, with his strong will, had set his heart on ministering in Asia Minor so firmly that it was hard for him to hear the call to Macedonia. After days of frustration and false starts, Paul came to the place of divine vulnerability. He was open to hearing anew from God, and then the Lord spoke. Frustration was transformed into direction; confusion became renewed commitment and understanding.

But may I say as forcefully as I can that Paul would never have gotten to Troas and that divine time in his life

IF HE HAD BECOME BITTER ABOUT THE CIRCUM-STANCES HE FACED. He would have been locked up somewhere in Asia Minor, mad at God, in a personal jail cell of self-pity. Circumstances may not seem like things that need to be forgiven, but they can become incredibly personal at times. Our choice is the same as it is with in-dividuals: Will we forgive, not hold on to our woundedness, or build a cell of personal anger?

All the Luck?

Let me refer to one other example who pulls together everything I have been saying. He is not an individual from the Bible, but see if you can identify him anyway. He failed in business in 1831; was defeated for the state legislature in 1832; failed in business again in 1833; ran and was defeated in his bid for House speaker in 1838; was defeated for Congress in 1843 and 1848, and for the Senate in 1855 and 1858; was rejected in his bid for Vice-President in 1856.

Have you identified him yet? He was Abraham Lincoln, the sixteenth President of the United States, elected in 1860.

"You know, some guys have all the luck in life." How often I have heard such a comment, but it is never true. Yes, individuals may have money through family connec-tions. Others may have physical good looks. But all the external things of life fade and disappear under the pressure of daily living. *Personal character* only increases with time as you make a choice not to be controlled by circumstances or destructive attitudes toward other people.

Our lives are not controlled by the "breaks" of life, whether negative or positive. As we yield our life to Christ, He takes the very points of our pain and turns them into qualification points for ministry. If Paul had not gone through the frustrations of Asia Minor, he would never have arrived in Philippi. The struggle that Abraham Lincoln faced as he moved toward the presidency uniquely prepared him to lead a country in the midst of civil war.

The Point of Greater Strength

Shoestrings do break in life. At times the very strings of our heart are snapped in the pressures of living. Things and people just don't work out to our pleasure and liking. We have several choices at that point: We can get mad at the shoe of circumstance; we can get mad at ourselves because our whole life seems to be a series of broken strings at critical times; we can even get mad at someone else (possibly our mate) as he or she asks, "What happened?"

But the answer in all these situations is to let the Lord tie the ends together. The amazing thing about a knot is that it becomes the strongest part of the string!

Paul approached the Lord concerning a point of breaking in his life. He lifted the strings of a troubling situation in his life to the Lord. The response he received is important for us to hear: "My grace is sufficient for you, for power is perfected in weakness" (2 Corinthians 12:9).

Paul responded back to the Lord in verses 9 and 10 by saying, "Most gladly, therefore, I will rather boast about my weaknesses, that the power of Christ may dwell in me. Therefore I am well content with weaknesses, with insults, with distresses, with persecutions, with difficulties, for Christ's sake; for when I am weak, then I am strong."

Please don't hear Paul sounding like a mournful man. He is not playing the martyr; he is not having a pity party. In fact the very opposite is true. I see him rising to his feet with a renewed sense of vision in his heart.

Paul understands that it doesn't matter how many times the string breaks—the Lord will mend the situation as I yield it to Him. The Lord is so sovereign and loves me so deeply that He will take this pain, this person, this situation, and turn it into a point of strength for me. No prison of the heart and mind of man can stand against the love of God.

6

Coming Out of Hiding

For many people the story of Samson sounds like a rerun of their own life's story. They have agonized in the clutches of sin and habit patterns which ruined their lives. They have known the embarrassment of public failure and ridicule. Yet for other people the story of Samson is foreign territory. They have never made such a notorious spectacle of themselves. Their existence bears an outward semblance of order, and they are attempting to follow the Lord. Yet inside they are living lives of quiet desperation. They are experiencing failure, frustration, and lack of fulfillment on the INSTALLMENT PLAN. The payments may be lower, but the interest will kill you. It just keeps adding up until there is nothing to do but hide from the pressure.

We can hide in various ways, such as procrastination. We just assume that if we never get around to doing the thing we fear, then maybe it will go away. We can hide in our work. The difficulties at home can become so great that we hide by pouring ourselves into our work. This method of hiding also carries the benefit of being very socially acceptable. Who can find fault with such a hard-working, honest man? The wife may hide by pouring herself into the kids rather than face the situation with her mate. We can even hide through the bluff. One of the most common bluffs for men today is to be "macho." Yet behind that tough exterior frequently lies a gaping chasm of self-doubt. The outward toughness only masquerades the inner confusion, but the tragedy is that soon his roughness desensitizes his soul. The man hides so well that he loses touch with himself. It is not that he doesn't want to feel and be sensitive but that he no longer knows *how* to be sensitive. The macho mode is so operational in his brain that he is stuck in numbness. He becomes trapped in the press of his own escape.

Hiding in the Winepress

In Judges 6 we meet a man caught in a unique press. Gideon is hiding in an abandoned winepress. Winepresses during the period of the Judges were usually constructed out of a series of rock-hewn pits. In other words, Gideon was hiding in a hole in the ground. Yet the winepress is symbolic of where he is spiritually: He is hiding from the oppression of the Midianites, who were particularly humbling to Israel.

It is clear from the narrative that the Midianites did not live in Israel on a continuous basis; they appeared in a cyclical manner, once a year. The problem was that their appearance always coincided with harvesttime. They roared in off the desert, bringing all their relatives with them, and ate everything in sight. It was like going downtown to buy groceries each week and being shoved out of the way by a motorcycle gang as they stole everything on the shelves along with your paycheck.

The nation of Israel had been under such treatment for

six years without making any serious effort to resist the Midianites. The people of Israel had simply sought hiding places for their crops in caves and dens in the mountains.

There have been few times in the history of Israel prior to the Babylonian captivity that the people of God have appeared so weak. Gideon would seem to be just another grape being crushed by the feet of the Midianites as we meet him in the winepress. Yet he was GOD'S MAN IN HIDING. In fact he was so well-hidden that he did not even know who he was!

> The angel of the Lord came and sat under the oak that was in Ophrah, which belonged to Joash the Abiezrite as his son Gideon was beating out wheat in the wine press in order to save it from the Midianites. And the angel of the Lord appeared to him and said to him, "The Lord is with you, O valiant warrior." Then Gideon said to him, "O my lord, if the Lord is with us, why then has all this happened to us? And where are all His miracles which our fathers told us about, saying, 'Did not the Lord bring us up from Egypt?' But now the Lord has abandoned us and given us into the hand of Midian."
>
> And the Lord looked at him and said, "Go in this your strength and deliver Israel from the hand of Midian. Have I not sent you?" (Judges 6:11-14).

Fearful Hero

I find myself chuckling every time I read this section of Scripture. One of the great virtues of Scripture is the fact that it presents the heroes of the faith without any cover-up. We see Gideon, for example, in all his timidness. Yet there is an intriguing honesty in his questioning of God's activity among the people of Israel. He dares to openly question the idea that God is blessing His people. He looks at the mess he is in and wonders what is going on. Good question!

The angel's response to Gideon's questioning is downright humorous once you understand the scene. Here is Gideon preparing food inside a winepress, beating out the few grains of wheat he has. It is an extremely difficult task because wheat is normally processed while standing in an open area. The grain is thrown gently into the air and allowed to separate from the husk. But because of his fear of the Midianites, Gideon is down inside a winepress, struggling to process what little food he has. Fear can make the simplest task difficult!

I'm sure that as he pounded out his lunch he was muttering under his breath over the situation. The questions which he expressed to the angel were but verbalizations of what was previously going through his mind. In the midst of all his anguish he hears someone say to him, "The Lord is with you, O valiant warrior." I am positive that Gideon's first reaction would have been to look around in the winepress to see who the angel was talking to. It obviously could not refer to him, for he was hiding for his life. He was a timid, frightened man—not a valiant warrior.

Avoiding a Challenge?

Yet the angel persists in his statements. Gideon tries to avoid the issue by bringing up the questions which had been troubling him concerning God's promise for Israel. But the angel will not be deterred. In verse 14 he repeats the initial statement and even challenges Gideon to deliver Israel. But Gideon tries to avoid the challenge again:

> And he said to Him, "O Lord, how shall I deliver Israel? Behold, my family is the least in Manasseh, and I am the youngest in my father's house" (verse 15).

Not in the least deterred, the angel responds by saying:

> "Surely I will be with you, and you shall defeat Midian as one man" (verse 16).

Little did Gideon know that the angel's promise was more literal than figurative, for he would defeat the vast hordes of Midian with just 300 men!

It becomes apparent as we read through chapter 6 that Gideon is not talking simply with an angel. The angel is referred to as Lord. He receives worship. He touches Gideon's offering and it is totally consumed by fire. There is little question that we are dealing with an appearance of Christ. As with the birth of Samson, Christ has come to be involved in the salvation of His people.

It is important that we take note of how Christ came. He came as a traveler, carrying a staff. And He sat under the oak tree, watching Gideon. He would be unnoticeable to those around Him. Isaiah put it well: "He has no stately form or majesty that we should look upon Him, nor appearance that we should be attracted to Him" (Isaiah 53:2). Isaiah is obviously referring to the incarnate appearance of Christ, but there is a principle here concerning the character of Christ: *He will never force His presence upon us.* Yes, there will come a day when He shall rule the nations with a rod of iron, but until that day He stands beside us, frequently unnoticed in the winepress of our problems.

Traveling with the Leader

The early Christian church had two important images which were used to explain the life of faith. The first was a figure of Christ; they consistently saw Him as a Shepherd. You don't find the cross appearing with any predominance in Christian art until around the fourth century. Instead you find Christ appearing as a tender Shepherd carrying a lamb draped around His neck. The actual figure comes from Greek and Roman art, but the concept is radically Christian. The early Christians were not drawn from the great artisans of society but from the common man. Thus there was a natural borrowing of contemporary art forms.

In my office hangs a reproduction of one of the earliest

representations of Christ we have found. It comes from the catacombs in Rome and pictures Christ in classical Roman clothing as a Shepherd gently carrying a lamb on His shoulders. The early Roman Christians obviously didn't need a picture of Christ on the cross because they frequently faced the possibility of being nailed to a cross themselves. They needed a Shepherd.

The second figure used by the early church fits with this concept of Christ and helps us to understand the nature of the Christian life. It is the figure of a pilgrimage. Life is a pilgrimage. Augustine, an early church theologian, pointed out the fact that we are on a pilgrimage to the City of God. The great classic *Pilgrim's Progress* of a later era also vividly illustrated this truth. Obviously the truth became distorted in the later traditions of the church as the pilgrimage became a process of getting to God rather than realizing that God in Christ has come to us. But the truth remains that we are all on a pilgrimage. Our problems don't ease when we come to Christ; I am sure you have noticed that! But the joy is that we finally have some answers.

Life of Frustration?

Recently a young married man poured out his heart in my office and finally in total frustration came to the point of his agony. With tear-filled eyes he looked intently at me and said, "Ever since I became a Christian nothing has gone right for me. The guys at work even kid me about it. They say they would never become a Christian if it means having my rotten luck." Here was another Gideon beating the sides of his winepress. "Where are the miracles that You promised, God? How come everyone on the Christian talk shows gets the miracles and all I get is deeper into a mess?"

I love questions like that, and I know that Jesus does too. Some Christians feel committed to live lives of hidden frustration. It is not nice to ask God such questions, but if we keep quiet we end up playing a Christian charade. The motions are there, but they are not real. We end up marching in place, and the pilgrimage of faith becomes a parade which circles the same block.

We need to realize that asking questions of Jesus and listening for His reply always brings the miraculous into our lives. The problem is that we are so frantically pounding the sides of the winepress of our problems that we can't hear His reply. The voice of our fellow Traveler, our Shepherd, is lost in the frenzied noise of our efforts to salvage what little we have left. Those few grains of wheat that remain became my total focus. Survival becomes the key issue. But mere survival is never the issue for the Christian, no matter how severe the circumstances. Christ said that He would never leave us or forsake us (John 14:18; Matthew 28:20; Hebrews 13:5). Basically we play a rigged game: We win no matter what, if we continue in the pilgrimage (Colossians 1:23). The problem is that we are looking at the grain instead of God, and we miss the voice of the Traveler in our efforts to survive.

What then is the solution? It is the same for us as it was for Gideon—a change in focus, a change from a survival mentality. However, the transition can be difficult. The transition for the young man in my office was difficult because Jesus was asking him a rather pointed question. In the midst of his struggle, his motives for following Christ were being challenged—for personal gain or out of relationship. It's a difficult question but also a loving question because it turns our heart back to our first love, serving Him.

Running from Despair

Two men on the road to Emmaus faced a similar question. They were in deep despair over the death of Jesus. They had so hoped that things would have turned out differently, but the crucifixion had ended their dreams. They were on their way to hide from the events that had transpired in Jerusalem, and in the midst of their bitter journey a Traveler joined them (Luke 24:15). The Traveler began to ask them why they were so troubled. Then He began to reprove them from the Scriptures concerning their lack of understanding.

Once again Christ, our fellow Traveler and Shepherd, is challenging some "grain-watchers." Little did the men know that it was necessary for the grain of Christ's life to fall into the rough ground of Calvary that all people might have life. Subtly these men had shifted to survival because they had not realized God's purposes in the midst of their circumstances. It was only as the Traveler broke bread with them that they realized that they had been speaking with Christ all along. Once again Christ had pulled men out of a winepress of personal despair.

In John 21 we find Peter impetuously throwing himself overboard in response to a Traveler who calls to him from the shore. John identified the Traveler as "the Lord," but none of the disciples ventured to ask the Stranger who He was. Peter had seen Christ after the resurrection. He had heard Jesus challenge Thomas to touch His nail-scarred hands and look at His wounded side, yet Peter returned to fishing.

It was not an act of belligerence; it was instead an avoidance of his calling. I'm sure he heard the words of Christ echo in his mind as he fished: "I will make you a fisher of men" (Matthew 4:19). As Peter pulled yard after yard of empty net into the boat, those words must have haunted him. He was a man hiding in the activities of daily life from the call of God. But the results are always the same: emptiness, lack, and a total absence of the miraculous in one's life. No wonder Peter threw himself over the side of the boat! Those fishing nets were killing him!

Much has been made of the details of the discussion between Jesus and Peter on the shore. There is a delicate dialogue in the original text between the Shepherd and

Peter concerning the flock. Jesus tenderly helps Peter discover again the love that they share. He calls Peter to respond out of his love for Him, and not to focus on the fact of his failure. The critical point is expressed in John 21:19: "Follow me!" "Peter, don't try to survive; focus on following me." But Peter is like many of us—hard of hearing—so he responds by questioning the Lord about the calling of another disciple. Jesus responds again by telling Peter to stop looking at others: "You follow me!"

Our meager grain can take many forms, from the actual kernels of wheat we have been hiding for ourselves to the comfortable yet empty grains of our past means of support. Both responses are failures through the installment payment plan. Both remove us from the fulfillment of God's purposes in our life. But above all, these responses fail to recognize the Traveler who has been with us even in the midst of our struggles. We bang and kick against the sides of our problem and all the while He is gently saying, "Surely I will be with you; have I not sent you?"

False Humility

In Judges 6 we not only discover Christ but we also see into the travail of Gideon. He is not only struggling over the bondage of his people, but at a deeper level he is agonizing over the humiliation of his position. I'm sure the questions he voiced to the angel of the Lord were doubts he had been muttering to himself all along. It's interesting to notice the sequence of accusations that come from his lips. They start with charges against God but rapidly become statements of self-incrimination. At the foundation of many charges that believers and even nonbelievers bring against God lies the thorn of self-incrimination. I have seen this sequence often because in the pain of self-doubt there is a projection of guilt to the Person of God.

Gideon sees himself a lot like the man who goes to the psychologist. After many hours of counseling and analysis the psychologist presents the patient with the results of his investigation. The psychologist states that he has some good news and some bad news. The good news is the fact that the individual does not have symptoms of any complex. The bad news is that he is simply inferior. That is exactly the picture that Gideon has of himself.

Samson was constantly set up by the false view he had of himself. His bravado bluff of doubt repeatedly gave ample opportunity for the enemy to destroy him. But Gideon took the opposite approach and chose to agree with all the enemy's accusations. Gideon would be called honest by some who emphasize the sinfulness of man, but such an approach to self is always counterproductive. It makes you piously miserable. It also sets you up to hate God and be of little threat to the enemy.

This view of self is not only counterproductive, but at the core it is unbiblical. I am constantly amazed at how many people preach Buddhism in the guise of Christianity. The believer is admonished to die, to crucify himself. The implication is that once all desires and passions are extinguished, then the person will truly be spiritual. He will be removed, and only Christ will remain. This is a lovely definition of Nirvana, the Buddhist concept of heaven. Nirvana is where you come into a perfect state of blessedness by the extinction of the individual. This is brought about by the removal of all desires and passions and by the absorption of the soul into the supreme spirit.

Pardon me, but Christ is not Buddha. He did not come with a giant eraser to blot out our personalities. He came that you might truly be "you" in Him. Apart from Him we have no life, but in Him we can truly be ourselves. We are called to recognize ourselves as dead to sin and crucified in Him (Romans 6:5-14), but not to crucify ourselves in Him.

The Deadly Threat of Legalism

Have you ever tried to crucify yourself? Messy, isn't it!

You always have one hand free no matter how hard you try. But if somehow you manage to finally crucify yourself by maybe pounding the last nail in with your forehead, you still lose because your *self* did it. This is the deadly threat of legalism. We fear our failures so we make up a code of rules that we can live by to deal with our sins. We end up pounding in the nails of a well-ordered life with a hardened heart. In our effort to be right with God we form a system of things not to do so we can please Him. We watch out for the evil of other people's hearts, but we know that at the core we are not doing very well ourselves because we struggle sometimes so hard to keep clean. We are the least in our "tribe" because we know that no one else in the church could possibly be travailing with such sin and weakness.

You can see many Gideons faithfully pounding out grain in the back of the church. They love the Lord but view themselves as second-class citizens in the kingdom. Miracles are something that happen in other people's lives, not theirs. They feel alone and sinful because of the doubts that they struggle with. Their thoughts are sinful at times, and they assume that if they really loved the Lord these kinds of things would never enter their mind.

As a result of all these pressures and false expectations of themselves they are driven to hide. Yet the great Shepherd of our soul is always calling us out of hiding. He is always drawing us nearer to Him, and in the process we begin to realize that He is not troubled by our sin. He even died for us while we were yet sinners. That is not just a one-time experience, for His blood continually speaks at the point of our fallenness.

The Vicious Hook

As we have previously pointed out, there are primal patterns within all of us which cause us violent mental confusion. In Genesis 3 we saw the fall of man which began with accusations against God. It was a small step for Adam but a giant step over the cliff for mankind. The serpent with incredible craftiness stated a devastating lie: "For God knows that in the day you eat of it your eyes will be opened, and you will be like God, knowing good and evil" (Genesis 3:5).

There is a vicious hook in that statement which is to embed itself deep within the mind of man. It is a multifaceted hook, for it not only accuses God but brings man to the point of questioning himself. If by eating the fruit man can be as God, it implies he is incomplete before doing so; Adam and Eve are not all they could be at present. The pattern is set: The heart of man is being violated with a false perception of self. Alienation is beginning. Man is learning to dislike himself as well as to distrust God. Soon man will leave a contorted trail through history as he endeavors to establish his identity apart from the purposes of God.

You can sometimes spend years ministering to certain individuals attempting to help them understand the love of God, but it is an arduous task. The difficulty comes from the fact that we are constantly dealing with their shattered self-image and the lies of hell which constantly attack their self-worth. Yet God the Father has been seeking since the fall of man to get man to love himself because *He loves them*. Lasting personal value comes from Him—not from our natural abilities or our successes, or even from any loving thing we have done. This alone is why we can face failure with confidence. We don't need to hide as Gideon or muscle it through like Samson. We have value despite our successes or failures. The cross of Christ forever speaks of the horror of sin, but even more importantly it proclaims the value of man.

Painful Improvement

As you listen carefully to the dialogue between Christ

and Gideon, you begin to notice that the Lord is responding to him with both affirmation and correction. Some
people would make the Person of Christ so meek and mild
that His lordship becomes synonymous with politeness.
Christ died for us, and Christ loves us, but it is a love that
responds so strongly to us that it will confront us. Notice
Christ's statement to Gideon: "Go in this your strength . . .
have I not sent you?" (Judges 6:14). It is not a courteous
suggestion from a gallant God; it is a corrective admonition expressed from the heart of a loving Savior.

Several years ago a friend presented me with a plaque.
On the plaque was a quote, but it was not from the Bible.
It was instead a simple statement composed by the student to express how he was doing in his pilgrimage. With
unadulterated clarity it expresses a common experience
of many hiding pilgrims:

> The truth shall make you free. But first it shall make
> you miserable.

How many times I have seen the truth of that statement!
Obviously it is not the whole truth, but to the Gideon hiding
in the winepress of failure and low self-worth it sure feels
like it. Initially truth is very painful for a Gideon. It faces
him with the necessity of change, which can be very
threatening. For example, time after time I have seen individuals seeking marriage counseling revolt at the possibility that maybe they need to change. The problem is with
their mate, not with them. Their mate needs to change,
but not them.

Responding to Change

A Gideon may not always be timid. Sometimes he can
appear to the casual observer as a confident individual.
Yet you always see the depth of an individual's self-worth
and personal confidence *by the way he responds to
change.* If he understands the nature and depth of God's

love for him, he can easily respond to correction. If he is troubled with himself, change can be a frightening adversary. But Christ loves us so much that He will not leave us struggling in our winepress of fear, no matter how strong a front we may project.

In a way there is a little Gideon in all of us. We hide in a variety of ways prior to meeting Christ. We learn to compensate for our perceived weaknesses with mental patterns of the world. These patterns allow us to function, but the cost in terms of personal anguish, destructive interpersonal relationships, and loneliness is devastating. There is no peace. It is failure on the installment plan. The problem with these mental patterns or programs of response is that we usually don't recognize them, or if we do see them the results of our actions so frustrate us that we strike out against the problem and usually reinforce the pattern. As we have discussed previously, there needs to be a yielding up of the patterns of our perception.

It is in those moments in the winepress of life's frustrations that those patterns are uniquely yielded. In the midst of the pain and frustration, if we would only put aside the noise of our anger or pity and listen carefully, we would hear the voice of the Shepherd gently correcting us. Our fellow Traveler is always ready to speak in those moments and give us direction—direction which helps us reprogram those ruinous perceptions of ourself, other people, and Him. But we must be willing to hear, because the correction can come through the most unlikely sources. The truth is divine, but the vehicle can be most mundane.

A Prayer That God Answers

Fortunately for me, the truth of this process of following Christ was deeply imprinted on my mind at an early stage in my walk with Him. I had just returned from Vietnam and had been marginally "born again." That is to say, Christ had come into my heart, but He was a long way from being Lord of my head and emotions. The amazing thing was the fact that I didn't realize it.

One evening my wife roped me into going to a prayer group. I can't remember much of the evening except that I didn't understand what was going on, and they asked me to pray. The group was small, so I figured it wouldn't hurt to try praying out loud. I can remember distinctly two older ladies bowing their heads beside me as I began praying. I wasn't going to be intimidated by the group, so I just said what was on my mind:

"Lord, whatever the hell you want us to do, we are open for it." Needless to say, the room became very quiet. I looked up and one of the precious old saints was visibly white. The other lady, not taken aback in the least, just leaned over to me and said, "Son, that was a good beginning. Would you like to learn a prayer that God always answers?" Well, I couldn't pass up an offer like that, so I said, "Sure what is it?" She replied by saying, "Just ask Christ to show you what He would like to change in you so you can be more like Him."

Deep within my heart there was a desire to follow Him. He had won my heart, and I knew that following Him wasn't just a one-time experience. I truly wanted to be like Him even if it demanded change.

Your Sword Is Jammed!

Little did I know that in a short time I would be facing a major turning point in my thinking about Christ, myself, and other people. The next day was a change-of-command ceremony at my naval training squadron. These events tend to be elaborate exercises in boredom: You end up standing for hours waiting for a few minutes of significant activity. Fortunately for me, I had been asked to serve as the adjutant to the commanding officer. It was a duty that I enjoyed because I would get to present the squadron to the new commanding officer. The actual reporting is usually accompanied by a sword drill. I considered myself to be very proficient at close-order drill and was looking forward to showing the new commander my stuff.

As usual, the preparation for the ceremony took forever. Being a Marine, I was convinced that the major problem was getting several hundred sailors to march in any kind of order. As I rather impatiently waited in the sidelines for my cue, I remembered the prayer the precious old saint had suggested. I didn't have anything else to do, so I asked the Lord to go ahead and reveal if there was anything He might want to change.

In the midst of the prayer the adjutant's call sounded and I marched forward. With great precision and force-fulness I began the process of calling for the squadron to report in. I was beautiful. The new commanding officer was duly impressed. With a final flurry of voice, Marine dress whites, and sword, I reported the squadron to be all present and accounted for.

Upon receiving the commanding officer's dismissal, I began the process of returning to the sidelines. My first task was returning the sword to its scabbard. This is where the story gets interesting. The Marine officer's sword is curved, and so the scabbard is also curved. It goes without saying that the sword and scabbard need to be curved in the same direction in order to fit into each other. Well, somehow in the flurry of activity the two had become mismatched. As I attempted to return the sword into its scabbard it simply would not go. The harder I tried the worse the situation became. As I looked at the commander, his face was turning bright red. His only response was, "Your sword is jammed, you fool!" This only increased my frenzied activity, which resulted in the scabbard falling from my side to the concrete floor. Finally, in total frustration, I picked up the scabbard and slowly crawled offstage.

The squadron was in pandemonium. As I stood with my shoulders slumped forward, with the sword in one hand and the scabbard in the other, I could not believe this was happening to me. The sailors behind me were coming unglued. They were literally bent over, doubled up in laughter. My world had come to an end!

In the midst of all that disaster I heard a still, small voice. It simply said, "See what an arrogant man you have become; but I would make you a lover of others." I knew it was the Shepherd of my soul. I knew it was in direct answer to the prayer I had just uttered. My first impression was that I should have never prayed that prayer in public! But at a deeper level I desperately desired to be transformed. I was a Gideon who had taken his winepress and armor-plated it. I had put it on wheels and built my own little tank of life. I decided to try to be the toughest guy on the block. The problem with that option is that you take the pressure with you. The stress of the press stays right on you. My tank had finally hit a divine wall. It was more than a wall—it was a mirror, and I could see clearly where I was headed.

The Winepress of Pride

I could respond to this incident in two ways. I could deny the whole thing and work harder on my sword drill. Of course denying something that the whole squadron was now laughing themselves silly about would be difficult, but I could try to tough it through. The other option was to turn to Christ and let Him change me. This would require that I change the way I thought about myself, my purpose in life, and other people. I was not called to be an arrogant little rooster but a lamb following the Shepherd of my soul.

I left something that day on the concrete floor of the aircraft hangar: I left a winepress of pride which had nearly squeezed the life out of me. I decided to stop hiding from my past—a past which had told me that I was less than everyone else, a past that said I needed to run faster than the rest of the pack to stay ahead. That day I heard the

Traveler call my name, in the midst of my frustration and pain, and say, "Give to others and I will be with you. You don't need to hide anymore."

As with Gideon, response to such challenges from Christ is difficult. My failure was of such dimension it was threatening to deal with. I made a commitment to let Christ change me that day, but it was difficult not to hide again. Time after time when I would encounter a sailor from the squadron, he would salute and grin and say, "Good morning, sir. How is your sword drill coming?" Ouch! Everything within me wanted to run back and hide in the old tough-guy tank, but instead I would choose to smile and say, "Better."

The years have passed since that incident, but the truth that I learned that day remains deep within me: Only Christ's presence brings peace in our lives. Only listening to Him can pull us out of our personal pits. Gideon left the winepress that day a changed man. The pain of the day, however, can be intense. It can feel like we are going to die, but God is faithful to bring us through.

Only Christ's presence will bring peace to our lives. Only time with Him will give lasting direction to our lives. It seems as we walk through life that we discover the lesson of His peace over and over again. The concrete floor of the hangar is no longer present, but the frustrations of life begin to feel a lot like a frenzied sword drill. Somehow the scabbard of the day doesn't fit with the curve of our soul.

Leaderless Battle?

Recently I had been speaking at several different churches over a period of a week's time. About the third night into the schedule I noticed a strange phenomenon: The words were dribbling out of my mouth, running down the front of my shirt, and lying in a pile at my feet. It was about as exciting as listening to a faucet drip. The congregation was kind, and they spent about 45 minutes watching the words pile up at my feet. After a short chorus we all went home.

We don't need to be in the pulpit to experience such struggles. The frantic schedule of a housewife or a businessman can bring us to this place of quiet desperation. The pile may be business letters or diapers instead of words, yet the effect is the same.

That evening I took Christ to task. I complained about all the time I had spent in His service during the week, and He wasn't even supporting me as I spoke for Him. Where were the miracles I had heard about?

In the midst of my pity party I began to sense the presence of the Lord. With the force of a gentle correction I heard the Shepherd of my soul say to me, "Isn't it interesting how much you have been speaking about Me yet how little time you have been spending with Me?" Now don't hear this as an admonition to get up at four in the morning and spend five hours in prayer. Jesus was simply pointing out that I had not been spending ANY significant time with Him. I had talked to Him about the day ahead. I prayed over my meal, but that was about it. They were prayers of necessity and not relationship. We can become a pilgrim roaring off to do battle with the activities of life, but we have no idea where our Shepherd is headed.

In our world we live at such a frantic pace: the noise, the interruptions, the deadlines, and the demands of daily existence. When you add to this the frequent feelings of failure and frustration that we all experience, it is easy for us to end up in a box canyon with Christ nowhere in sight.

Let the Lake Be Full

We live in a beautiful part of the West Coast. The Oregon countryside is a rich tapestry of velvet green fields and evergreen forests. One of the reasons it is so lovely is the high amount of rainfall we receive each year. Thus a lack of rain is a unique event in our neck of the woods. Several years ago we experienced a drought. In the midst of the drought I traveled back to several dams that lie in the high mountains above our home. It was an interesting experience. The drought had been so severe that the water level of the dams was extremely low. There was no overflow from them to the valley below.

But the most striking change I noticed was the smell. You could catch a hint of what you would see even before you came to the rim of the dam. There was an odor of decay, and as you looked down on the lake area you could see a small body of muddy water and a gruesome field of old stumps. What had once been a beautiful lake of clear blue water, surrounded by a field of pine trees, was now a ghastly mudhole surrounded by a forest.

How often we can end up feeling like that dried-up lake! It isn't so much that we walk in sin, but that we are always running instead of walking with Him. In our rush of activity we can let the lake of our lives be drained of His presence. We find ourselves experiencing a drought of business. In fact we are not even a dam at times—simply a canal. Bernard of Clairvaux, one of my heroes of the faith, put it well:

> If you are wise you will show yourself a reservoir and
> not a canal. For a canal pours out as fast as it takes
> in, but a reservoir waits till it is full before it overflows
> and so communicates its surplus.

Bernard died in 1153 A.D., but his words are as current as the morning newspaper. In fact I think they have become more relevant with the passing years because we now live in such a fast-paced world.

The Ultimate Refreshment

In the process of the pilgrimage we can miss the important issue of life: following Christ and being refreshed by Him. As the lake of relationship drains we also find the stumps of past struggles sticking up all over the place. Areas which we have dealt with years ago begin popping back up. We feel the pressure to hide or jump back into our armored tank. The patterns of past perceptions rise up in our emptiness to plague us.

That night I discovered afresh the need for my mind to experience a daily washing from the patterns of the past. Without it I easily revert back to old ways of thinking. Our patterns of perception lie deep within us, and sometimes it takes years for the roots of those old stumps to finally be removed. Yet Jesus is our Shepherd. He will come to us even in the mudhole of fatigue and business. He will call to us in the despair of our winepresses. He will even lean into our tanks of defensiveness and help us get our sword untangled.

He is constantly turning our mistakes and times of emptiness into miracles of refilling as we lift our hearts to Him. He can even help us to fail forward out of the winepresses.

7

The Backyard Battles
Of Life

In our study of the call of Gideon we saw him struggling with the issue that so many of us face—a perceived
lack of ability. In the pit of the winepress Gideon came to
grips with the issue of God's call on his life, and his own
ineptness. But the angel of the Lord didn't just say that
He would be with him; He also *commissioned* him. He
didn't just call him; He also *commanded* him. I find myself
chuckling at the call but wincing at the command. The command is too close to home. In fact, it deals with our
backyard.

> Now the same night it came about that the Lord said
> to him, "Take your father's bull and a second bull
> seven years old, and pull down the altar of Baal
> which belongs to your father, and cut down the
> Asherah that is beside it; and build an altar to the

> Lord your God on the top of this stronghold in an
> orderly manner, and take a second bull and offer a
> burnt offering with the wood of the Asherah which
> you shall cut down" (Judges 6:25,26).

This passage of Scripture sounds very strange to the Western ear because of the various cultic gods and idols that are mentioned. Yet the scene is amazingly relevant once we understand what is taking place. Gideon's father, Joash, has built an altar to the pagan god Baal. Beside the altar stands an Asherah, which is a wooden female fertility goddess. Analyzing the situation in modern terminology, we would say that Gideon's dad has a fairly pornographic backyard!

Tear Down the Altar

This altar apparently had been in existence for quite awhile, and the surrounding countryside viewed it as a holy place. More than likely Gideon grew up in the sight of such an altar, and it had become part of the daily life of the community.

Yet the command from the Lord is to tear down his father's altar. Not only is Gideon to tear it down, but he is to use his own father's bull to accomplish the task! The Lord is asking for a serious case of CONFRONTATION. Gideon is facing a backyard battle.

Generally we focus upon the great contests of life—the issues that bring into conflict large amounts of either people, political forces, or money. That is why there is usually such an interest in the specific details of the battle between Gideon and the Midianites. But I believe the critical points of Gideon's character were forged not as he faced the Midianites but as he responded initially to the commission of God in his life.

We determine destiny in the backyard battles of our life. For many people failure always seems to happen to them, but not to others. But the truth is that success or victory is not determined so much in the arenas of major conflicts as it is in the nitty-gritty of backyard confrontations. The great successes come as a result of commitments forged in daily battles.

Winning on the Home Front

In the challenge of his father's backyard a Gideon was formed. The Lord had called him to be a deliverer of Israel, but the first person who needed to be delivered was Gideon himself. He had to face the contest with the family altar before he could ever take on the Midianites.

Nor is this contradictory to what we have said previously. Our emphasis has been to underline the fact that *you cannot handle failure by just trying harder*. You can't reach down and pull yourself up by your bootstraps when a failure or mistake has literally blown your shoes and socks off. There is nothing to grab except your toes! It is only by the grace of God that we have our life and being. Only He can put the broken pieces together.

Yet His grace calls us to *respond*. All the facts we have discussed concerning the nature of our emotions, the character of our mind, and the love of God will be useless to us unless we respond. We have to face the backyard battles of our life and *respond to our commission in Christ*.

Paul expresses this vividly in Philippians 2:12,13:

> Work out your salvation with fear and trembling, for
> it is God who is at work in you, both to will and to
> work for His good pleasure.

I remember the first time I ever heard a sermon on this passage. The preacher must have been mad at someone, because the only word I heard was "fear." He ranted and raved for 40 minutes on how we had better perform for God—"we ought to"; "we should." Yet right in the middle of his diatribe I began to see the meaning of the text "God is at work in you." Christ is for me! He is working in me! He truly is *with* me, not *against* me!

Out of the fact that God is at work within us Paul calls us to "work out" our salvation. The term "work out" carries a beautiful meaning within this context. It literally means to dig out or mine something. The Greek geographer Strabo used the word when he referred to Roman mining operations. No one reading Strabo's letter would suppose that the Romans were *acquiring* the mines; rather, they were *exploiting what was already securely in their possession.*[11] Whenever Paul uses the term "work out" in his letters he always refers to the finished work of Christ, not something waiting to be acquired by the believer. We are called to work out the unsearchable riches which we have received in Christ Jesus.

Worshipful Theology

It is not easy to see how God's sovereign love in salvation and man's free agency as a creature in God's universe can coexist, but they do, according to the Scriptures. We can reason through the various elements of the Christian faith, but at the very core of every central issue of the faith lies a mystery. Jesus is fully God and yet fully man. The triune nature of God is a mystery: God the Father, God the Son, and God the Holy Spirit. And we are faced with a mystery in the sovereign love of God and the free will of man.

"Work out your salvation!" Paul is calling me to respond to the infinite love of God. There are certain things that God will not do, and one of these is to force us to be all that we can be in Him. His purpose is to bring us into relationship with Him, not just to get us to heaven. He challenges us to *respond to Him*, to come and walk with Him.

Mining the Riches

I was flying over southern Texas one night years ago.

The student pilot was in the rear cockpit of the fighter aircraft. My job was to monitor his wanderings across the airways of the Southwest and to foil his frequent attempts at killing both of us. In a moment of unique compassion I took pity on him and adjusted the aircraft so that it would literally fly by itself. As we winged our way back to our home base, I leaned back in the ejection seat, put my feet up, and just looked up at the vast panorama of stars overhead. The student was busy in the backseat, under the instrument hood, trying to figure out why the plane was not falling out of the sky anymore, so I had several moments of peace and quiet.

At 30,000 feet, in the middle of night, you can see forever. The Milky Way was a virtual highway of stars arcing over the aircraft's canopy. I was looking at a pathway of hundreds of billions of other stars which are part of our little galaxy. Due to the fact that we were passing over a relatively uninhabited area, the infrequent lights on the ground below seemed to blend into the panorama of stars overhead. I was suspended in a sea of God's creation. I was overwhelmed by the immensity of it all, and aware as never before that the One who created all of this died for me. I made a commitment that night to respond by His grace to His love. I wanted to be all I could be for Him. Little did I know that many backyard battles lay ahead for me. I was to face many idols which I had subtly grown used to. I was to begin the task of mining out the riches of Christ.

Do We Have Idols?

Idols are interesting objects in the Old Testament. They take a variety of forms, from the imposing gold image of Nebuchadnezzar's day (Daniel 3) to small household idols (Genesis 31:19). They seem strangely remote to us and our way of thinking. The idea of having a stone image sitting in our backyard seems completely absurd. Yet they become amazingly relevant once we realize that an idol is simply AN IMAGE WHICH REPRESENTS A SPIRIT.

If you had asked Gideon's father why he believed a piece of stone was a goddess, he probably would have laughed at you. He was not worshiping a stone, but rather the goddess which the stone represented. The wooden idol was a point of reverence for him, something that he bowed toward. He needed the assurance that his crops would be fertile and productive, and this goddess supposedly could provide that for him.

Yet idols are as common today as they were in Gideon's time; they have just changed from stone to mental images. Satan is still carving idols today, but they are in the minds of men. They are mental images which cause a believer to bow down, to give deference to someone or something other than the Lord.

Satan's tools for the construction of idols are subtle and varied. Over years of counseling I have seen him carve on the minds of men with many tools, but certain ones are used repeatedly.

The Blade of Hostility and Anger

This is a subtle instrument because the individual feels that he is actually in control. The temper flares. There is an explosion and the blade cuts deeper, and with each response the pattern deepens until the person is no longer consciously choosing to be angry; he just is. Many times I have heard a young lady say that she can't stand her mother and will never be like her. Yet this very hostility is day-by-day forming her into a carbon copy of the very person she wars against! She is being controlled by her anger. She is bowing down to the bitterness of her own soul.

The Press of Fear and Anxiety

All of us deal with anxiety and fear in some dimension,

yet unless we face this adversary it can control us. It becomes a pressure which causes us to bend our knee to circumstances rather than to the Lord. The enemy takes the point of our fear and constructs a situation which soon dominates our very life.

The Hammer of Doubt and Negativism

Like a sledgehammer pounding upon the soul of man, the adversary can use the natural tendency of fallen man to question God as a point of condemnation.

Some of us were born into a family which added pessimism to the baby formula. When the comedian cries, "I can't get no respect," we know exactly what he means. The love of God for us personally is a difficult concept to grasp on a daily basis, and the enemy is quick to point out our doubt to us.

The Grind of False Guilt

Guilt is a significant motivating force within man. Even in our own society, which has so rejected the commands of a loving God, you see individuals attempting to be free from guilt. They are like Pilate washing their hands of accountability, yet all the while their very acts cry out for a means of forgiveness.

Satan will even take the redemptive force of guilt and grind idols of condemnation within the hearts of men. He uses the rules and regulations of men to generate a false guilt which defies cleansing. False guilt produces a bondage that defies forgiveness. Satan can even take the fact of Christ's forgiveness and say that we can no longer sin once we have been forgiven.

We cannot take the love of God and gauge it by the love of men. If we do we end up classifying ourselves as second-class citizens in the kingdom of God.

The Mold of Inferiority and Inadequacy

Few tools are used as constantly by the enemy as inferiority and inadequacy. These form a paralyzing mold which some Christians force on themselves. They have not yet seen who they are in Christ, and they literally tear pieces off themselves to fit into the crippling mold that the enemy has handed them. Their own mistakes and failures stand in their mind as vivid confirmation that they are truly inadequate in the game of life. The trap of comparing themselves with others becomes a constricting vice which locks the mold ever tighter around them. They are saints under constriction rather than saints under construction, and life is slowly squeezed from them as they bow before the false image of who they are.

Idols of the Mind

With tools such as these the adversary of our soul constructs idols of the mind—mental images which control us and restrict the expression of Christ within us, images which frequently lie within the "fault lines" of our personality. They may not be visible to the casual observer because they reside within the fissures of our being. Yet under pressure they surface, and we respond to them without even thinking. We bow in the urgency of the moment.

The fault lines of our personality are not points of explicit sin, but they set us up to respond to sin. They are fertile areas for the construction of mental images which control us rather than the love of Christ. The cracks and fissures can come from a multiplicity of sources. One such source is the sting of childhood rejection which questioned our worth and sets us up to constantly compete against other people to gain value. An abusive authority figure at some point in our life who inflicted a deep wound leading to a seedbed of hostility within us is another source. The causes may vary but the result is the same: a fracturing of wholeness within us, and the potential for bondage.

Because these fault lines frequently lie within the points of our woundedness and are not made of stone, they are difficult to see. We bow before them as part of our daily liturgy. We find ourselves saying, "That is just who I am. It is part of my family trait. I have always been hotheaded." After awhile we begin to believe such statements and no longer even notice that they have become a point of bondage.

How much like Gideon we can become! The idols which surrounded him were fixtures of family significance. They had become part of his personal life. They were so much a part of him that it must have come as a shock that the angel of the Lord would even make such a request.

"The idols? Oh, yes, the image of Baal and the Asherah in the backyard. But I don't see what that has to do with me conquering the enemies of my life." But you find out how important they are when you begin to deal with them.

> Then Gideon took ten men of his servants and did
> as the Lord had spoken to him; and it came about,
> because he was *too afraid of his father's household
> and the men of the city* to do it by day, that *he did
> it by night* (Judges 6:27).

I love Gideon's response—it gives me such hope! The point we need to notice is the violent struggle which Gideon faced. The idols of our life resist change with a vengeance. Frequently we cannot even see them, and so we cannot simply sit down and analyze our lives or a particular recurring situation and decide to get better.

Am I saying that analysis is useless? No. What I am saying is that apart from revelation and the grace of God we don't get very far even in our best efforts.

We Have a Helper

Christian character is not a result of joining the "try

harder" club. We are not saved by grace and then developed by grit. In Romans 8, Paul gives us an insight into the answer for our blindness. He speaks of the continuous ministry of healing which takes place in a believer's life as he follows the Lord:

> The Spirit also helps our weakness; for we do not know how to pray as we should, but the Spirit Himself intercedes for us with groanings too deep for words (Romans 8:26).

Just as the angel of the Lord pointed out Gideon's weakness, Paul says that the Holy Spirit is helping us with our weaknesses. The word "weakness" carries a wide variety of meanings, from physical sickness to emotional struggles and even to *timidity*. In fact, one of the central emphases of the word focuses upon the emotional life of the believer.[12]

Gideon is a classic example of someone riddled with the weakness of timidity. He is cowering in the winepress for fear of the Midianites, but the angel of the Lord sets him free by pointing out the idols in his backyard. Many people would have given him a tongue-lashing instead and pointed out his lack of faith. They might have brought up the fact that many people had died for the faith and he needed to toughen up. Some might even have given him a pep talk on thinking positively. He just needed to start thinking right. He was one of God's chosen people. These Midianites were trespassing on the land that God had given to the people of Israel, and so he had authority over them. Both of these approaches contain a modicum of truth, but they will end up with one result: having a lot of camel tracks all over your back. The backyard idols must go before we can defeat the oppressor. First things first.

"The Spirit helps our weakness."

I almost shout with joy every time I read that verse. As a counselor I have seen time after time how faithful the Lord is to point out hidden areas of bondage in people's lives. He helps us to see the backyard mental images which bring the people of God under subservience and cause us to be less than we can be.

The Double-Check Complex

She was a perky young lady, full of life and the love of the Lord. Yet there was a certain sadness in her eyes, a hesitation in her step. Something was missing in the total picture. As we sat in the counseling office together, we discussed a problem she was experiencing at work. She was employed in a department store as a clerk. Her job entailed the recording of various accounting records, and she was frequently behind in the processing of those records. This was a source of great personal embarrassment to her. She could add the required column of figures quickly but found herself constantly reviewing her addition. In fact, there was a sense of constant review about everything she did. It never seemed to be good enough. We obviously were dealing with a struggle over the issue of self-image, not just accounting skills.

After an extensive time of discussion, it became apparent that the struggle was deeply ingrained within her. Telling her to pray more, to read her Bible more, and to "whatever more" would be of little help. She was fighting an enemy that she could not see, and she needed to recognize her adversary.

Frequently when sincere Christians fight violently with crippling habits or perceptions of themselves, we are dealing with previous mind patterns. Normally in the process of walking with Jesus we are healed of previous perceptions. As we come into an understanding of His love for us the shackles of the past fall by the wayside. Yet occasionally the shackle is more than a restriction; it has given birth to domination. It has taken on the proportions of an idol in our life. As we pull up the chain of restriction, attempting to identify the point of blockage, we come upon an incident in the past. The enemy has gilded and lifted up the event as a point of control for the individual: It has become an idol of the mind.

This young lady was bound by such an event. The sin of another person can deeply entangle us if we let it control our lives, and she had been entrapped by such an incident. In the first grade, as she was diligently working on a math assignment, the teacher observed her making a careless mistake. In an instant she grasped the little girl by the nape of the neck. As the wayward child hung suspended in midair, demeaning comments about her intellectual abilities were unleashed on her. They burned deep within her little soul. Once released, the aggrieved young lady was to carry that incident with her for years. Each time she added a list of numbers in her mind, the teacher was present to evaluate her performance. No wonder she double-checked everything! A childhood incident had been built into an idol of domination.

But the Lord's word for her was the same as it was to Gideon: "Pull down the altar. Don't let anything but my love control your life. I am the One who died for you. Don't let another person determine your value. Don't let your boss, your mate, your circumstances, or your failure control your life. I am the Lord your God who heals you."

She began a process of urban renewal that day, redecorating the corridors of her mind. Our mind is not a debating hall but a picture gallery, and sometimes we place the most destructive pictures in places of honor. Jesus came that day and helped her move the incident from a place of honor. It was no longer to have a place of domination in her life. She began the process of reordering her backyard according to God's perspective.

Wrestling with God

We can react to the various wounds of life in a number of ways. The young lady had responded through acquiescence. Others can react through aggression. In my first year of seminary I found myself in one of those wrestling times with God, fighting with everything yet desperately hoping I would lose. There was a dryness in my life. The winds of doubt were howling across my soul and the grinding grit of daily life was getting unbearable. It seemed that Christ had come to give me life, and life more miserably. Yet I knew the difficulty was not with Jesus; it was with me. I just didn't want to admit it.

I didn't know exactly what the problem was. Yet if you had asked my wife, she could have given you a detailed description of the difficulty: It was a plain and simple case of pride—pride that was invisible to me, but choking out my very life and my relationship with other people. Many times my wife had started to point out the problem, but she was wise enough to know that if she changed me I would just revert back in a couple of days. She needed to have the Lord change me, so she decided to cry out to God on my behalf.

As I was walking down the corridors of the seminary one day, thinking of all the things I needed to do, the Lord spoke to me: "Why are you still wearing military clothing?" I thought it was a rather silly question, so I ignored the inquiry. Yet it came to me again with renewed force as I walked. I knew it was the Lord. In typical fashion I presented all the justification for my action. I was a student living on a limited income; I couldn't afford to get a whole new wardrobe. But the problem was not economic; the problem was pride. I knew deep within me that I was wearing those clothes out of a reactionary sense of pride. Ever since I had returned to the United States, I had experienced nothing but subtle rejection from other people because of Vietnam, and inside me roared a fire of deep anger. The clothes were a statement of personal pride and frustration.

I was still struggling with nightmares over friends I had left behind and the insanity of war, and if nothing else I was going to at least hold onto my past. Yet with the love that only the Shepherd of my soul could express, I heard the Lord say for me to get rid of the clothing. It had become *an idol of identity for me*. I was finding my value in what the clothing represented instead of in Him.

The Turning Point

I remember telling my wife of the decision. The look on her face was priceless—a combination of relief and puzzlement. She knew the difficulty was pride, but what did military clothing have to do with the problem? Yet the Lord is the only One who can untangle the Gordian knot of our past. He and He alone knows the depths of our soul.

Did getting rid of the clothing release me from my bondage to pride? Not totally, but it was a significant turning point. As I lay aside the symbols of past perceptions and turned to Him, the nightmares faded away. I was no longer struggling for identity. Christ had become my point of identity. My purpose was to serve Him, and He could even make sense out of the hell which I had seen and the rejection I had faced. In the years ahead I was to face points of pride repeatedly, but the tide had been turned. I could learn new ways of responding to life. I could learn new ways of thinking about myself and others because of His love for me. The idol had fallen and the bondage had been broken.

You may not have faced an irate teacher or the insanity of war, but is there an area in your life which quietly yet powerfully controls you? It could be a temper you have struggled to control, a physical habit which defies you, fear or depression which seems to be a frequent companion, or overwhelming timidity in social situations. The details of the problems may vary but the effect of the idol is always the same. It controls an area of your life. You are dealing with a backyard battle.

The servants of the Lord are called first to the backyard

battles of life if they are to experience victory in this life. The question of whether you are going to heaven is not an issue; the question is effectiveness in this life. The catch is that the backyard battles are not easy. They face us with two unique challenges.

Being All That We Should Be

For some of us it is easier to commit ourselves to some great cause, especially if public notoriety takes place, than to take the lesser position. "Lord, I want to go to Africa to serve others!" may be our cry. And the Lord replies by saying, "No, you stay at home, serve others, and deal with your pride." "But, Lord," we reply, "then no one will see me."

Others may struggle like Gideon with timidity and be afraid to come out of the winepress, grumbling like crazy but stuck in mind patterns of personal intimidation. The Lord will gently confront us with the need to move, to change, to start tearing up the backyard.

In either case the challenge is one of commitment to be all that Christ calls us to be. The challenge does not come at the points of our strength but at the fault lines of our personalities, the very place where the enemy loves to build altars of domination.

How often I have chuckled with other brothers as we have shared our lives with one another. Time and again I find gentle, loving men and women struggling with Christ's personal exhortations for them to become more assertive in their lives. Others are constantly hearing the voice of Christ saying to be more sensitive. We are all being brought to a balance point of wholeness in Christ, and the critical issues are faced in the backyards of our lives: at the places where public acclaim is not given; at the places where it is not natural for us to obey; at the places where commitment to Christ is spelled out in the sands of daily life.

Transformed Forever

How difficult it is to live a supernaturally natural life with the people who know us so well! How difficult it is for us to still have faith after we have faced the onslaught of a well-meaning friend or relative! We share with them how Christ has promised to change us, only to hear a re- hearsal of our past failures. This is especially difficult in long-standing husband-wife conflicts. The husband or wife makes a commitment to change, only to catch from the mate the subtle scent of sarcasm, which saps the very life out of their efforts.

It is in these backyard battles as nowhere else that we discover the supernatural power of God for ourselves if we understand two things: the nature of God and the nature of faith. With respect to the nature of God, we need to see that God is the God of the impossible. I have had the great joy of seeing many miraculous healings—of people who physically had no hope, yet in a moment of divine intervention had health replace disease and despair replaced with joy.

However, over the years I am beginning to see that the greatest miracles are not the *physical healings* but the *character transformations* which occur as we walk with Him. A physical healing will affect an individual for as long as he lives physically, but transformation of the heart lasts forever. We take only two things out of this life: our character and our relationships. Everything else is left behind.

The human personality can be incredibly stubborn. On the other hand the supernatural love of Christ is incredibly transforming. At times we may unconsciously classify certain people as unchangeable, only to have God break through in their lives and totally amaze us. He truly is the God of the impossible. Because of His character, we can ask for the impossible—a transformation of us and our situation.

Realistic Faith

Please notice the mental state of Gideon as he responded to the Lord. He tore down the altars in the middle of the night because he was scared stiff of what his father and the men of the city would do. It is also important to remember that Gideon is listed in the Hebrews "hall of fame." With these two facts in focus we can see the nature of biblical faith: Biblical faith is put into action when you and I hear or perceive a point of obedience to the Lord, and even though we feel like running or doing something else, we choose to respond by obeying. It is when you do something in the middle of the night because you are too scared that God says, "Well done, faithful one."

I don't know how many years I lived under a crushing and unbiblical concept of faith. I had this picture in my head of how someday I would be this great man of faith. I would be a man who never doubted, never struggled, and constantly walked in absolute confidence. I would just speak, and lightning bolts would fly off my fingertips.

After several years of frustration it finally dawned on me that I was waiting for a feeling which had little to do with faith. Faith is not a demonstration of *fearlessness* but of *obedience*. It is not a *struggle to believe* but an *act of obedience to Christ's love*.

Gideon was a man of great faith because he responded wholeheartedly at his point of obedience. He chose to be command-oriented and not circumstance-controlled. His knees may have been knocking but he kept moving forward, and it was in his backyard that the attitude of obedience was born. He was to face the hordes of the Midianites, but it was no more frightening than the anticipated wrath of his father he faced that night.

A pattern was broken that night—a pattern of domination which had infected Gideon's family. A pattern of *obedience* was born that night, a pattern of liberty which would not only set Gideon free but also his family and the nation of Israel. Idols cannot stand in the face of obedience to the love of God.

Now we find the results of Gideon's obedience:

> Then the men of the city said to Joash, "Bring out your son, that he may die, for he has torn down the altar of Baal, and indeed, he has cut down the Asherah which was beside it." But Joash said to all who stood against him, "Will you contend for Baal, or will you deliver him? Whoever will plead for him shall be put to death by morning. If he is god, let him contend for himself, because someone has torn down his altar." Therefore on that day he named him [Gideon] Jerubbaal, that is to say, "Let Baal contend against him," because he had torn down his altar. Then all the Midianites and the Amalekites and the sons of the east assembled themselves; and they crossed over and camped in the valley of Jezreel. So the Spirit of the Lord came upon Gideon (Judges 6:30-34).

This section of Scripture is loaded with action! All the central issues of the narrative are coming to a climax, yet two results stand out vividly. These results underline the supernatural process of the transformation which is taking place. The first transformed person we encounter is Joash! He was the very person that Gideon feared the most, and yet *he was transformed into his greatest defender!* We don't know the exact reasons for Joash's change, but we do know that Gideon's obedience is directly connected to that turnaround. Our adversaries are affected by our obedience to the Lord.

Miraculous Turnaround

My friend Julio Ruibal was an evangelist in South America. After a very successful time of public ministry, he found himself suddenly being detained by government forces of the country in which he was speaking. He was being held captive in a remote area and was surrounded by hostile-looking guards. It didn't take long before Julio was struggling with fearful thoughts of what would happen to him. He knew he would probably disappear without a trace. Right in the middle of one of those fear fights he was having with himself, a gruff-looking guard motioned for him to get up and follow him. After a short trip down the corridors of the detention building he was shoved into a bathroom. It was a small bathroom, and he found himself jammed into one end of the room with the guard glaring at him from the other. Julio was sure he was going to meet his end in this remote bathroom.

The guard looked intently at Julio and asked him if he was the man who healed people. He was totally taken aback by the guard's question, but managed to blurt out that he didn't heal anyone, yet knew Someone who did: Jesus Christ. The guard then ordered Julio to pray for him.

With very little effort Julio was able to pray with great intensity! When our life appears to be on the line it is amazing how intense we can become! As Julio began to pray he realized he was not only praying for the guard but was dealing with a personal limitation of fear. We can discover our backyard idols in the most remote places!

After he had finished praying for the guard, Julio waited to see what the guard's response would be. He simply looked at Julio with tears in his eyes and asked if he could know Jesus. They prayed together and the guard was beautifully saved. After a short pause the guard drew his pistol again and motioned for Julio to come out of the bathroom. He was escorted back to the room and brusquely ordered to return to his seat.

The guard had been touched and had given his heart to the Lord, but Julio was still sitting in the midst of a fearful situation. Yet the situation was not the same, because the Lord had turned one of Julio's enemies into his protector. In a few hours Julio was to walk away a free man from that potentially disastrous situation, and it was due largely to the transformed guard.

We can all identify with Julio's fears, though we may not be as gifted as he is. We have all faced times of deep inner turmoil where the thing we feared appears to be pressing in on us. Yet if we respond in obedience, even weakened obedience as Gideon, we will find that the Lord will be our defender and even touch our adversaries in the process.

Stretched by God's Love

Obedience to the directions of the Lord with respect to our backyard battles can not only transform our adversaries but also penetrate the social relationships around us. Joash was not simply an adversary; he was Gideon's father. Obedience to Christ can not only transform our enemies; it can deeply affect our families. It has such an impact upon our family relationships because they are the ones who know us the best. They know our weaknesses intimately. They have to live with them on a daily basis. So when the idols are torn down they realize that something radical has happened. Maybe our relatives would respond more readily to us if we concentrated more on our need for change instead of demanding that they change. Obviously we want our loved ones to know the grace of God, but frequently our demands only drive them further from knowing the Lord.

There were two results in Gideon's life as he responded to the Lord: His father was changed, but even more important, *Gideon was changed*. In Judges 6:34 we find a unique expression of that change:

> So the Spirit of the Lord clothed Himself with Gideon, and he [Gideon] blew a trumpet and the Abiezrites were called together to follow him.

I have translated the verse literally for you so as to catch the graphic illustration presented by the author. Gideon was literally stretched by the Holy Spirit. The experience of dealing with the backyard idols was frightening for Gideon. He faced enormous pressures in the task, but by the grace of God he obeyed—and in the process he was transformed. We no longer find him grumbling in the winepress. He is instead calling the people of God to face their enemies.

The task of the church has never been to have large buildings. It is not even to have large congregations. It is instead to have LARGE PEOPLE, a people who have experienced the divine stretch of failing forward when they would much rather run the other way.

Gideon truly is an encouragement to us all. There is, however, one category of failure which we have not discussed that transcends even the pain and pressure which Samson and Gideon faced. It is the abyss of feeling that God has failed us.

What do you do when the Traveler by the oak tree is nowhere in sight? When a prayer for renewed strength only brings divine silence? What do you do when God fails? In the next chapter we will face this crucial question.

8

What Do You Do When God Fails?

Pastoral counseling is an exciting challenge. It is not so much a matter of in-depth psychological analysis as it is giving life away. The input of psychological research is helpful at times, but apart from the Holy Spirit people just learn to modify their behavior. They don't really change. They just rearrange who they are.

One of the beautiful things about the ministry of the Holy Spirit is the fact that He is not restricted to a certain type of setting. You don't need the stained-glass beauty of a church sanctuary to get the right mood. You don't need the melodic strains of a church choir to have an altar call. The Holy Spirit is at work in every situation of life if we only have eyes to see and ears to hear. This is one of the reasons I love to counsel on a racquetball court. It gets you away from the inhibiting confines of a formal office setting and into the give-and-take of real life.

The Really Tough Question

One day I was sitting with a young man who had just come back to the Lord. We were both leaning against the back wall of a racquetball court desperately trying to regain our breath. The Holy Spirit can turn such times into moments of vulnerability, in which the deepest thoughts of a man's heart are expressed. The young man looked at me intently and bluntly asked, "What do you do when God fails you?" We had just been joking about various points of temptation that every man faces, but I could see by the expression on his face that the question was not in jest. There was a seriousness in his eyes, and from his past I concluded that it was a question of deep personal significance.

What would you say to the young man?

Would you point out to him that Scripture clearly states that God never fails us?

Would you rebuke his unbelief?

Would you say that in time he will come to see that God is at work in every event of his life?

All these responses have validity, but I doubt if they would have helped that young man. It is a tough question to confront. We can easily give various responses which deny that the problem exists, but to this young man and many others it is a burning issue.

There is no doubt that from the biblical text that God is omnipotent, omnipresent, and whatever "omni" you want to call Him. Yet from our perception there are times in our lives when God has failed us.

I am not speaking of the simple frustrations of life in which our prayers go unanswered, when things just don't work out the way we expected. I am speaking of the times when we have faithfully obeyed and believed, but things only got worse. The problem with the whole situation is that we got there by FOLLOWING GOD.

The Room with No Exits

We can learn to handle our own failures. We can work through the dungeons of self-defeat and the winepresses of despair. We can even learn to live with the failures of other people and the restrictions they impose upon us. But at the point where we perceive that *God* has failed us, we enter a room with NO EXITS.

For most of us the question of God failing us passes with time. We keep going, and eventually the situation resolves itself. We sense His love again, so we simply go on and file the problem under the category of "unidentified flying incident." But for some of us the incident becomes a crisis of giant proportions.

The problem or question of God failing us can become particularly crushing for a committed Christian. They are almost obligated to not question the character of God, and so their perception of God failing them is repressed. The difficulty with repression is that it soon leads to *expression*—in some very destructive ways. I have frequently found myself sitting across from another brother or sister who has committed their life to Christ. They have served the church with distinction, yet we find ourselves discussing the fact of their fall into immorality. Those are very awkward moments for me, because I sense the individual's need for acceptance, but I also sense his need for correction.

The one point of correction I always find myself addressing is the inner attitude. Without exception, every person I have ever counseled who has fallen while serving the church is hostile. They are frequently unaware of that fact, because they are actually angry at God. They deny that they are angry at the conscious level because their theological system will not allow them to face this fact, so the frustration is just shoved under the carpet. The only problem is that the lump under the carpet soon fills the house, and life becomes intolerable.

The hostility toward God may not have caused the fall. It may be a *result* of the fall, but healing never comes until the question of God's perceived failure is faced. The question asked by my friend leaning against the back wall of the racquetball court cannot be avoided. It cannot be lightly brushed aside by an appeal to the fine points of systematic theology. Systematic "anything" doesn't help much when your life has just been blown apart and God appears to be the Culprit.

He Faced the Same Question

The Bible's answer to such a question is not a systematic defense of the character of God. It is instead the presentation of someone who has faced the same question— someone who has faced the dark night of the soul and discovered instead the infinite depths of God's love. Such a man is Hosea. He was a man who faced the pain of believing God failed him. He felt the sting of public ridicule as his hopes literally disintegrated before his very eyes. He faced the tough questions of life.

Hosea was a prophet to the nation of Israel. His prophetic ministry began during the prosperous and peaceful years of Jeroboam II, and closed as the Northern Kingdom moved toward its tragic finale. You will remember that the nation of Israel had broken into two warring camps after the kingship of Solomon. The tribes to the north, known as Israel, formed a separate state. It was to this wayward group that Hosea was called to speak. He served for more than a quarter of a century in the Northern Kingdom, and his is the only prophetic writing in Scripture that is exclusively from the north.

The uniqueness of Hosea is not found in the fact that he came from the north but rather in his distinctive emphasis. Time and again commentators are struck by the fact of Hosea's New Testament focus.

> It is amazing to find in this Old Testament book so
> much of the New Testament message and to find the
> basic call of the true evangelist. Every note is there.
> Every area is uncovered. Every appeal is sounded.[13]

This New Testament focus can be synthesized in one word: *hesed*. *Hesed* is one of the Old Testament words for love. Hosea's main cry concerns the love of God for His people. Yet it is not an easy love, because this cry of love is expressed in the midst of a violently sinful people. The love of God lies in direct conflict with another concept which throws Hosea's life into painful tensions: the harlotry of a nation. The ministry of Hosea is a statement of God's love in contrast to the lust of Israel. The word "harlotry" occurs in either noun or verb form a total of 27 times in the first nine chapters of the book. Six times we hear Hosea speaking of Israel's "love" in running after false gods. We are listening to a nation caught in the stranglehold of lust.

It is amazing how contemporary some Old Testament books become when compared to American life today! We are in the midst of a culture gripped with lust—lust for power, possessions, and the other person.

God Is Not Bound

Our focus right now is not the challenge of lust, however, but the question of *our response when God seems to fail us*. We find an answer to this question in the midst of the book of Hosea, because in the agony of Israel's sinfulness God chose to express His character through Hosea. Prior to this expression of character we read of the preparation of Hosea, and we discover a man who faced the pain of God failing him.

> The word of the Lord which came to Hosea the son
> of Beeri during the days of Uzziah . . . . When the

Lord first spoke through Hosea, the Lord said to Hosea, "GO, TAKE TO YOURSELF A WIFE OF HAR-LOTRY AND HAVE CHILDREN OF HARLOTRY; FOR THE LAND COMMITS FLAGRANT HARLOTRY, FOR-SAKING THE LORD!" So he went and took Gomer the daughter of Diblaim, and she conceived and bore him a son (Hosea 1:1-3).

I capitalized the command of the Lord to Hosea so that it would catch your eye. I doubt if there are more startling words in the Old Testament. There are many disturbing acts in the Old Testament, but they usually come from sinful men attempting to respond to the Lord. Yet in this verse we have the Lord commanding one of His prophets to marry a harlot.

It is interesting to read the various commentaries at this point. I am constantly amazed at the lengths to which people will go in an effort to cover God's supposed mistakes. Even hyperconservative authors shudder at this verse and go through various grammatical gymnastics in an attempt to rewrite the text. Their basic supposition is that God would never do such a thing.

Long ago I learned that God doesn't live by man's limita-tions. Hosea didn't marry Gomer and afterward she became a harlot; God told him to marry a harlot. This chapter is also not simply a parable or fictional story to il-lustrate a preaching point. It comes out of the sweat, blood, and tears of Hosea's personal life. It speaks of the agony of a man who knew the pain of God's heart. But he discovered the heart of God in the midst of his own per-sonal pain.

The Prophet's Stormy Marriage

"Go, marry a harlot." I am sure that the command rang in the ears of Hosea. Like a hammer against a sheet of metal, it must have reverberated within him. But we have not only the command but also the reason: "For the land commits flagrant harlotry." This helps us to understand the command and Hosea's reaction. Essentially Hosea doesn't hesitate. He marries Gomer and begins to have the back room painted for the little one who is on the way. Yet if you read through the rest of the chapter it becomes apparent that things go rapidly downhill. The first child is clearly stated as being Hosea's, but soon the origin of the ensuing children is not even mentioned.

The climax of the struggle is expressed in the final child's name, "not my people." The implication is obvious: The people are not God's and the child is not Hosea's. For six long years Hosea watched his wife continue in the path of personal destruction. I'm sure that many nights were spent in sleepless anxiety over the missing Gomer, for he knew that she was returning to the ways of her past. He became a prophet of God married to a woman who constantly threw herself in the arms of other men. This would not be a problem for a pimp, but it was living hell for a prophet.

He had willingly married her in response to the command of God. It was to be an illustration of God's love for His people. Hosea knew of the love of God. He knew that if he poured his heart into Gomer, she would leave her past life of destruction and follow him. Hosea and Gomer would then illustrate God's redeeming love for Israel. He would prophesy of the love of God with the evidence of Gomer standing beside him. But now he was nothing more than the brunt of coarse jesting as he moved through the streets of the city. Hosea was a man tasting the pain of life; even more humbling, he was faced with the fact of apparent divine failure.

The Crisis Point

How often I have seen this scene repeated in life! A man or woman takes off with the Word of God burning in his heart. They feel destined to take on a difficult task.

It could be the transformation of a marriage, the establishment of a Christian business, a call to the mission field—whatever. They are not dreaming. They have heard the Holy One of Israel. Six weeks, six months, or six years later they drop out the other end with teethmarks all over them, and just to add insult to injury they see someone else right next to them greatly blessed of God. Behold, another potential Hosea. It is a crisis point which anyone can face as he or she walks with the Lord.

It is a crisis point of belief,
a crisis point of understanding the heart of God,
a crisis point of obedience in a disobedient world.

The passage in Hosea is so troubling because we are seeing a man in the middle of open-heart surgery, a man brought to the crisis point of trusting God in the midst of personal pain. It is so easy to become unbalanced at this point. No one in his right mind enjoys pain, and so we go to extreme lengths in our reaction to biblical incidents which clearly illustrate moments of agony in life.

Some individuals respond to pain in other people by saying that if they had more faith they would not have the difficulties they are experiencing. Others react by seeing life as nothing more than an excursion tour of pain punctuated with moments of peace—kind of a spiritual endurance contest. The first view brutalizes people to fit a particular theological slant. The second gives you a brutal God. Either way you lose.

Love Without Limits

Several years ago I was sitting with my son in the backyard. It was a tense time for the two of us. He had involved himself in some activity that was unredemptive, to say the least. I was frankly upset at his blunder and on the ragged edge of applying the board of education to the seat of his pants. As I looked sternly at him, his little chin began to wobble and big tears began to stream down his face. He knew that he was in serious trouble. I had just pointed out to him that if such an action occurred again he would definitely not like the consequences.

Then without even hesitating, I heard myself saying, "But I want to tell you, son, that nothing you do will ever cause me to stop loving you. My love for you is not open for question. I love you no matter what!" I stopped after making the statement and realized that this was the same way my heavenly Father loves me.

God the Father loves us without limits. He is *for* us, not against us. He will never leave us or forsake us in Christ. We are His children. However, we must understand that in this life the Father disciplines His children (Hebrews 12:5-11). Please notice I said *discipline*—not punish. He forms us through the disciplines of life. Sometimes it is in the personal agonies of life that we come to the deepest lessons of His character.

He disciplines us, and He doesn't have to play by our rules. He is Father God, and we don't decide how we should raise ourselves. We could choose as a rebellious child to go our own way, to live a life of rejecting His loving corrections. We could reject the pain of forming and correction, but with this choice we receive the destructive pain of self-rule. The question of dealing with God failing us *is always a question of parenting.*

Where Is God When I Need Him?

Can we trust our heavenly Father, who is far more loving than any earthly father, to care for us? The circumstances scream at us. Gomer has left us. She has not only returned to sin, but our life is totally ruined. Where is God when I need Him? Did I really hear the Lord say for me to marry her? Can I ever trust myself to believe His Word again?

Hosea's problem is not just the problem of a prophet;

it is the problem that everyone faces in the tragedies of life. The Christian divorcee faces the agony of a life torn to shreds by an unfaithful mate, and the question always comes, "Why, God?" The Christian businessman has his lifelong business disintegrate before his very eyes. It was a business that he had dedicated to God, a business that began in faith but is now in failure. "Why, God?"

The list is endless because we live in a fallen world, but the important fact is that the potential for restoration is even greater. We have a loving heavenly Father who can take even the agonies of our shattered expectations and use them to form us into the image of Christ.

In the question of "why" we come to the essential issue of the nature of God. Our pain defies description. It leers at us out of the wreckage of our life and we can't understand why it happened. If God is so loving and powerful, where was He when I needed Him? Corrie ten Boom, the young lady who hid Jews from the Nazis during World War II, was to ask herself the same question in a German concentration camp. In her later years of life she was to be greatly used of God in ministering to other people as she recounted the details of her dreadful days under the heel of her sadistic captors. Her response to those days of pain and horror is most informative. She never answered the question of "why" but responded instead by saying, "However deep the pit, God's love is deeper still."

No Immediate Answer?

Sometimes God doesn't answer the question of "why," and Corrie understood this. What do we do when it seems God fails? First of all we must move past the question of "why." In the Gospel of John the disciples saw a man blind from birth and asked Jesus, "Rabbi, who sinned, this man or his parents, that he should be born blind?" (John 9:2). Christ responded by not answering the question of why but pointing out that the limitation is actually an oppor-

tunity for the works of God to be displayed in the man
(John 9:3). Then He healed the blind man. In this incident we see the marvelous work of God in the midst of
our whys. It is interesting that in the process of the healing
Christ asked the man to respond. He asked him to wash
his eyes in the pool of Siloam. Whys filled with personal
pain seldom respond to logic; they need a personal
response of faith. Only on the other side of the issue do
we begin to see with new eyes.

We perceive a love that is greater than concentration camps;
a love that is greater than our expectations;
a love that is greater than our pain;
even a love that overwhelmingly conquers the
tragedies of this life.

As the blind man, we begin to perceive our world differently, but we also notice that we ourselves have been
changed. The process of struggling with the whys in life
not only changes our understanding of God but also
changes us. Many people have seen the book of Job as
a great dark cloud in the Bible. It supposedly is a story of
darkness, one in which the inscrutable God of heaven has
decided to pick on one of His servants. In reality we are
dealing with another blind man receiving his sight.

Generating Questions

Interestingly enough, the book of Job also has the highest
frequency of the word *hesed* in the Old Testament. It is
not a story of a raging, wrathful God but speaks instead
of the covenant love of God in the midst of the whys. It
is, like the story of Hosea, another incident of a servant
of the Lord going through open-heart surgery. The book
of Job not only reveals a man struggling with the whys of
life, and the covenant love of God, but also a divine
perspective on the Lord's dealing with one of His servants.

As we read the book, it is as if we have been given a seat in the stadium of Job's life. We watch with amazement at the interplay between God, Job, and Satan.

In Job 1:8 we find a statement which triggers a cascade of events in Job's life.

> The Lord said to Satan, "Have you considered My servant Job? For there is no one like him on the earth, a blameless and upright man, fearing God and turning away from evil."

If that verse doesn't generate a few whys in your mind I don't know what will! Why is Satan standing before God? Why does God challenge Satan concerning the character of Job? That is like waving a red flag at a bull!

In Job 2:3 the dialogue continues between God and Satan:

> The Lord said to Satan, "Have you considered My servant Job? For there is no one like him on the earth, a blameless and upright man fearing God and turning away from evil. And he still holds fast his integrity, although you incited Me against him, to ruin him without cause."

Job has lost all his possessions, and the Lord is still challenging Satan! Questions literally flew through my head every time I used to read that passage. Job is not a sinful man. He is righteous and turns from evil, yet all hell is breaking loose in his life and it appears as if the Lord is stirring up the entire situation.

Things don't get any better as the book progresses. Several supposed counselors appear on the scene. In chapter 4 Eliphaz drops by to give some advice. We could call him Eliphaz "the superspiritual." He has a vision and knows just what the answer is to Job's painful situation. He says that since the innocent never suffer, there must be something wrong with Job. Bildad bludgeons Job with his word of condemnation in chapter 8 by telling him that he is not seeking God enough. The troublesome trio is complete with the appearance of Zophar in chapter 11. Zophar the zealot identifies the problem as being sin in Job's life. With friends like these three you just don't need enemies! How often I have heard their opinions being fostered as the reason some brother is going through a difficult time in life. Yet the brother is just like Job, an upright man. Thus the expression of opinions only adds insult to injury as the suffering brother struggles with the justice of God.

God Is Involved in the Pain

Yet in all the agony we begin to sense that God is after something in the life of Job. He is forming one of His servants, and the scalpel of circumstances is probing deep within the heart of a man. From Job's perspective all appears to be lost; the Lord has abandoned him.

But the truth is that the Lord is intimately involved in his pain. In Job's response to God in chapters 29 through 31 we begin to see what the Lord is dealing with. In those three chapters Job begins to speak out against God, and in 96 short verses we find approximately 100 uses of the personal pronouns: I, me, mine. The issue comes to a climax in 31:35:

> Oh that I had one to hear me!
> Behold, here is my signature;
> Let the Almighty answer me!
> And the indictment which my adversary has written.

Job is making a legal accusation or complaint against God. He is taking legal action against God! He is attempting to drag the Almighty before a bar of justice.

Have you ever done that? I know I have. Job obviously is caught in a web of his own righteousness. He is indeed righteous in the eyes of the law, but his righteousness has become self-righteousness. Job's problem is not one of arrogance or willfully sinning. He is just self-righteous. How subtly such attitudes take root in the heart of man! In fact we frequently are blind to the deep things of our heart. Destructive attitudes can quietly become part of our mental processes and can cause us to slowly die by inches.

Listen When God Speaks

I remember an incident years ago in another racquetball game that I had played. It was a foursome, and my partner and I were not doing well. In the midst of the game I suggested several ways we could improve our play. It didn't do much good. We were thoroughly beaten.

After the game my partner approached me in the shower. I could tell something was bothering him. With neck muscles and veins protruding, he began to relate to me the point of his disturbance: It was me. With intense gestures and facial expressions he began to describe what he thought of my interpersonal skills. I listened as carefully as I could to the volley of accusations, and to tell you the truth I disagreed totally. We managed to part company without any blows being exchanged, and I simply considered the incident to be a result of my irate friend's hypersensitivity.

How easy it is for us to miss God's corrective actions in our daily life as we blame others for the conflicts we encounter. It is a subtle blindness which frequently lives at the points of our own personal prejudices or fears.

Yet in the divine timing of the Lord I was to attend a class in the next hour discussing the life and teaching of the prophet Isaiah. As I sat in the classroom the professor began to discuss the Suffering Servant's Songs of Isaiah. These are prophecies of Isaiah which describe the coming Messiah. I listened to Isaiah's description of Christ given approximately 700 years prior to His incarnation. I was totally fascinated. Isaiah had such a rich understanding of the coming Christ. I was moved afresh by the character of my Lord. The Suffering Servant's strength and compassion stirred something deep within me.

In the midst of this delicious academic discovery I sensed

the Lord speaking to me. He was challenging me to look back at the incident with my friend. I began a review process of the conflict, and in particular the game we had played together. In the review a unique thing occurred: I began to see the game from my friend's perspective. I saw what it looked like from his tennis shoes. I may not have said anything openly hostile to him, but the way I glanced at him was hostile. The way I attempted to dominate the game was demeaning to him.

As the Holy Spirit helps us with our weaknesses, He frequently shows them to us through the eyes of another. The open-heart surgeries of painful interpersonal relationships are at times some of the clearest visions we receive of who we can be in Christ. In the agony of honestly seeing our failures we also see with poignancy how far we have to go in becoming like Christ. Yet it is not a condemning vision. Rather He calls us to a renewed honesty and fresh commitment of our confidence in Him to get us there.

Dropping the Sword

Something broke inside me that day. I sat and wept in the back of the classroom over my deep need for healing. Yes, I had dropped my sword. Yes, I had gotten rid of the clothes of pride. But I was still saddled with habits and actions from my past. I could not even see them at times. I was blind at the point of my deepest need. In fact our relationship with Christ can actually become such a point of comfort for us that we subtly miss our need for change in the warmth of His acceptance. In His love He will even allow painful conflict and potential loss of friendship to occur just to get our attention. At times we go through this agonizing time of conflict so that we might discover our need for Christ in an entirely new way.

Obviously my loss was nowhere near the pain that Job suffered, yet the principle is the same. The "why" times of life give us a unique opportunity to see ourselves. What do we do when God seems to fail? First we need to get past the "whys" of the situation by the grace of God and then be open to see in ourselves points where the Lord is bringing wholeness despite our pain. Our reaction to the situation can frequently reveal areas of deep blindness. We find out what is inside the cup of our souls when disagreeable circumstances bump into us. The impact of unwanted circumstances can cause a spilling out of harmful thoughts, feelings, and attitudes that we have buried deep within us—thoughts that have subtly prevented other people from relating to us, attitudes that have quietly hindered us from drawing near to the Lord, and feelings that have eroded our wholeness in Him.

It is critical at this point that we balance this issue carefully. God is for you; He is not against you. Not everyone who is sick is in a Job situation. If we begin making those kinds of deductions, we are no different from Job's counselors. The Lord clearly states that the counselors misrepresented Him (Job 42:7), and His wrath was kindled against them.

Christ died for you and is committed to you. He does not ask you to perform to gain His approval. At the same time, however, we must never forget that He is Lord, and that He does not have to play by our rules in the pilgrimage of life. In fact, He loves us so much that He will discipline us at times in the details of daily life. We don't like this; it is distasteful to us; but at times there is no other way. Our blind spots sometimes become apparent to us only under the spotlight of personal pain.

The Mystery of God's Love

After Job completes his tirade in chapter 31, it is as if the book stands on tiptoes in anticipation of God's response. Finally, in chapter 38, after Elihu's comments, the Lord speaks. The response of the Lord is intriguing in several ways. The Lord doesn't answer the question of why, even though the reader clearly sees the forces at work behind the scenes. The next four chapters focus upon only one important issue: the character of God the Creator. The Lord answers the accusations by sharing of Himself. No identification of guilt occurs. No revealing of the heavenly conflict takes place. Instead you can almost hear the words of Christ's reply to the disciples concerning the man born blind. This is for the glory of God.

In the response to the revelation of the character of God Job cries out, "I have heard of Thee by the hearing of the ear; but now my eye sees Thee; therefore I retract, and I repent in dust and ashes" (42:5,6). Job beheld the glory of God in the midst of his struggle. He saw anew the character of God, and in the mirror of his personal pain he clearly saw himself.

Of equal importance in the Lord's reply to Job is the fact that there is no reference to legal language. The relationship between a servant believer and the Lord is not one of give-and-take or a business contract of mutual benefit. It is instead a relationship of God's sovereign grace. He who brought into existence all of creation has set His love upon men. It is a fellowship of grace, and grace is always greater than any "give." The lawsuit disappeared in the light of God's glory, and Job's claims on God vanished in the power of His presence. More importantly, Job moved from a head knowledge of God to a heart knowledge.

If you would look back over your lives, I am sure you would remember many joyous moments with the Lord, yet it is in the pain and frustration that we come to the deepest understandings of His love. He didn't extract us from each of the situations; instead He loved us through them.

Like Job, we may have gone through the surgery of having everything fail around us, including God, in order to come to an understanding of the blindness that lies within us. On the other side of the pain, we discovered that God never left us. He just acted in ways that were beyond our comprehension.

Real Light at the End

One friend of mine put it well when he said to me, "Last month I thought I saw the light at the end of the tunnel, but it turned out to be a freight train coming the other way." I laughed with him but understood that he had discovered more than pain. Then he paused, looked thoughtfully at me, and continued, "But I have come to understand that the light was there all along, because Christ was walking with me even in my blindness." We rejoiced together because he was coming to understand what Paul said:

> For I am convinced that neither death, nor life, nor angels, nor principalities, nor things present, nor things to come, nor powers, nor height, nor depth, nor any other created thing, shall be able to separate us from the love of God, which is in Christ Jesus our Lord (Romans 8:38,39).

God's love covers open-heart surgeries, times of personal blindness, and even moments when God seems to have totally failed us. NOTHING shall be able to separate us from the love of God in Christ Jesus.

Most of us never face the agony of a life like Job's, in which we lose family, friends, possessions, and health overnight. Yet even in Job's life we see that God is our Advocate, not our Adversary. He takes our ADVERSITIES and turns them into ADVANTAGES. The final chapter of the book of Job says that the Lord restored the fortunes of Job as he prayed for his friends. He not only restored his fortunes but increased them twofold. But far beyond the material blessings is the fact that Job came to understand the Lord.

God's apparent failures are only transitory. He never brings or allows a difficulty to enter our life that He does not intend to use as a stepping-stone to an open door of blessing—a door that could never have been opened any other way. The problem is that from our perspective the difficulty appears to be the death of us, and it looks like it will last forever.

Not Just a Private Choice

In the life of Hosea we also saw a situation in which God seemed to have failed—that is, from Hosea's perspective. This life situation is different from Job's in the fact that God was not after something in Hosea. Instead, He was dealing with the sinfulness in the nation that Hosea had been called to serve. Hosea's situation is by far the most common in life. The Scriptures say that believers are called to show forth the character of Christ in this world. Paul, writing to the believers in Rome, complimented them on the fact that their faith was being proclaimed throughout the whole world (Romans 1:8). Our faith is not simply a matter of personal importance. This is a very important truth for us to understand.

We as Americans tend to have some unique twists to our understanding of biblical faith, and one such idea is that our commitment to Christ is only a matter of individual importance. The Lord, however, is in the process of expressing His reconciling love to all men THROUGH US. In fact Paul clearly states in 2 Corinthians 7 that we are ambassadors for Christ and that God is entreating others through us. If we don't understand this calling in our life, then living will not make much sense at times and God will seem to fail us.

What do I mean? Look at Hosea, chapter 3. If you compare the beginning of chapter 1 with chapter 3, you will discover an interesting difference. The command of the Lord to Hosea starts off the same in both chapters but their content is radically different. In chapter 1, the Lord commanded Hosea to "take" a wife of harlotry. In chapter 3, the Lord commanded Hosea to "LOVE" a wife of harlotry. What a world of difference in those commands!

Sensing the Heart of God

Why the difference? The love of God was learned through the failure of chapter 1. Hosea learned about the love of God through failure. In chapter 2, he has come to *personally know* the love of God. A love that loves "in spite of." A love that doesn't carry conditions but is compelled by compassion. Job went through the surgery of having everything fail around him, including God, to remove his blindness. Hosea went through the surgery of personal failure to have something added to his heart.

The Losers of Life

The book of Hosea could have never been written apart from the experience of chapter 1. We need the Gomers of life—the failures which initially make no sense, but when yielded to Him bring us to a place of understanding the very heart of God.

The Gomers of life help us to understand ourselves. How easy it is to love the lovely, be they people or situations. We can easily believe God for great things when everything is going our way, but the Gomers help us to grow beyond ourselves. They drain us of our natural resources and force us to look to Him.

How difficult it must have been for Hosea to go to the slave market. Once again the public ridicule must have been withering. "Look, here comes the prophet to pick up his prostitute." The marketplace would have reverberated with raucous laughter. But I am sure that the market would have grown strangely quiet as the sound of Hosea's coins striking the seller's table filled the air. A holy hush would have settled on the crowd as Hosea approached Gomer and gently took her in his arms. She was a woman wasted in sin, lost in the destructive pattern of self-abuse as she sought for affection. And surrounding her was a nation lost in the same insane rat race of sin.

I doubt that the crowd could have explained what was taking place, yet deep within its soul it felt strangely moved by the parable of God's love which was appearing before their very eyes.

Trust Me!

Recently I found myself sitting in the parking lot at church. I was deeply frustrated with a situation in my life. It was painful to me, and there appeared to be no remedy. As I cried out to the Lord, I was taken back to a special time in my life, a time of decision and faith.

I was standing outside a roadside motel. I had been walking my dog after helping my wife unpack our car. We had just resigned from military service. We had sold many of our prized possessions and had committed our life to serve the Lord. I was to enroll in a seminary within the next month even though I didn't even know what a seminary was. I found myself looking at the night sky overhead, and watched the familiar outline of military aircraft heading back to the air base that we had just left.

Then it hit me like a ton of bricks: What was I doing out here walking my dog around a vacant lot, headed to a school I didn't even understand? I must be out of my mind! Maybe if I went back to the military on my hands and knees they would take me back. I had gone too far with this Jesus stuff!

In the midst of that frightening turmoil I heard the gentle voice of my Lord saying, "Trust me. I will take care of you. I will never leave you or forsake you." Many years had passed since that special night. I have grown greatly in the knowledge of the Lord and His ways among men. Yet there was a certain pristine relationship that was established that night. I settled the issue of who was really

Lord of my life. I set aside all the personal expectations of my life. I committed myself to follow Him no matter what.

The Lord took me back to that moment in my life to show me what I was dealing with. The situation I was struggling over was not the problem. God had not failed me. He had simply refused to be controlled by my agenda. In fact He had a better idea for me. I had taken all the promises He had given me in the last several years and placed them in what I thought was the correct order of fulfillment. I had made a time schedule for God, and now I was deeply disturbed at His lack of performance.

I needed to travel light again; we all need to constantly unpack. We need to return to the place where we can be more concerned about other people than about our personal agenda. We can become so consumed with personal fulfillment that we lose sight of the most important thing in life—following Christ. He doesn't operate on our time schedule. He isn't required to function according to our scheme. He is committed instead to bring us to wholeness and health under His gentle hand.

The Sense of Ultimate Victory

Once we face and walk through the tough question of "Why, God?" a unique thing takes place within us. To put it simply, WE BECOME UNSTOPPABLE. We may not be the swiftest runner in the pilgrimage of life, but there comes a deep sense of ultimate victory. We are unstoppable because we have nothing to lose. We have let go of our personal contracts. We are following the Lord. We are not responding to Him in resignation but in affirmation. We yield not because we don't care but because we care so much. He is Lord, and we are making plans and attempting to follow Him, yet we are learning to keep a loose hand on the control of the details of life. In the process we conquer the number one nemesis of initiative—the fear of failure. We learn to fail forward into His arms.

9

Victory Out of Failure

Earlier in this book we looked at the failures of some of God's "real people." We began our investigation by looking at the life of Samson. He is a classic example of CATASTROPHIC failure. The fallout of his life literally spews across the pages of Scripture, yet through it all we sense the Lord's deep love for him. Gideon was a COWERING failure, a man caught in the web of his own weaknesses, and yet the Person of Christ was to call him out to greatness. Finally, Hosea was a CARING failure. His concern for Gomer and the heart of God was to lead him into the agonizing position of appearing as a horrendous failure in the eyes of men.

No One Is Free of Failure

If you stand back and look at the composite picture of these men's lives, one thing immediately catches your attention: Failure is common to all of mankind; it is one of the universal experiences of humanity. Paul put it well when he said, "For all have sinned, and fall short of the glory of God" (Romans 3:23). We have all dropped our swords somewhere in life and have heard the loving yet firm voice of the Lord identify our point of need. We have all found ourselves wearing clothes of our own identity rather that the righteousness of Christ at times. I think everyone has at one time or another been involved in games with other people. It may not be an open physical conflict on a racquetball court. It may have been in a delicate yet vicious conflict over the leadership of a women's or men's group in the church. We like sheep have all gone astray at some point in our pilgrimage.

To further complicate the matter, other people frequently go astray right through the middle of our lives. They mess up our neat categories and stretch us past our ability to endure. They shatter our comfort zones as they recklessly drive through our lives. Life is filled with failures in one form or another for people who care. Therefore, one of the critical issues of life is learning THE VALUE OF FAILURE.

When I speak of the value of failure, I am not making a Pollyanna statement—you know, "the grin and bear it" approach. What I am saying is that in the texture of daily difficulties, God is at work if we have eyes to see. He is not only at work; He can take failures that are yielded to Him and turn them into our foundations. He even takes our mistakes and turns them into miracles.

As we pointed out earlier, some people view failure as a mere inconvenience in their upward climb through life. They deny the fiasco, and focus instead upon positive incidents. It is important that we view life from a perspective of faith, but faith is not denial; it is a clear recognition of the failure, a turning to God, and a belief that He is greater than our blunders. Our focus is on *Him*, and not simply on positive thoughts.

Sour View of Life?

Other people, including many Christians, have a sour view of life. Failure is just another nail in the coffin of their view of man. They perceive man as being totally corrupt. His heart is constantly twisting toward wickedness, and even the saints need to be watched. Their hand is nervously feeling their wrist as they take their spiritual pulse. It is a life of eternal insecurity. Failure is deeply feared and avoided at all cost.

The obvious difficulty in this view of reality is that our lives, like the men and women of faith in the Scriptures, are spotted with failures. Running from failure is trying to hide from yourself. It can only be accomplished through rationalization and eventual deception. As we have previously stated, the value of failure is first of all a confrontation with self. It is a growth in honesty.

Promise of Great Works

But failure has a value far beyond self-revelation. This is seen clearly in John 14:12, where Jesus makes the startling statement, "Truly, truly, I say to you, he who believes in Me, the works that I do shall he do also; and greater works than these shall he do; because I go to the Father." The promise is clear: Belief in Christ releases the miraculous, and the Lord even promises a partnership in the process! This is obviously not an equality of God and man, but a marvelous continuity of the expression of the life of Christ. Yet the greatest miracle of the passage to me is not the promise, but the persons addressed. Jesus is speaking to the disciples—the very disciples who would betray Him in a matter of hours! John 13-17 gives us a record of the final hours of Christ with His disciples. These hours are so important that John devotes one-fifth of his entire gospel to their presentation. In John 14:12 we find one of the central emphases of those parting words.

He turns to a Peter who will in a few short hours deny that he knew Him; yet He says, "You will do the works I do."

He looks at a Thomas who will initially reject the fact of His resurrection; yet he says, "You will do the works I do."

He shares His heart with a John who will silently watch as He is crucified; yet He says, "You will do the works I do."

They all would deny Him; yet He says, "You will do the works I do."

Christ's words speak to us clearly of the fact that human failure is not a limitation to God. His disciples would all betray Him, and He knew it, yet He spoke of their ultimate victory. In these words we discover that the greatest value of failure for us personally is the rediscovery of God's grace. Grace for the contemporary Christian is much like the manna that God provided for the children of Israel in the desert: It is our daily bread; His grace is fresh for us each morning. In fact we grow to expect it; we get up in the morning and don't even think much about it. But the joy of our initial walk with Jesus slowly dims, and, like the Israelites, we soon learn to grumble about the inconveniences of life. We partake of the daily grace of God but forget the miracle of its provision.

Suddenly on the horizon of our life comes the challenge of failure—either the impact of personal failure or the fallout of the mistakes of others. In those moments, with our body embedded in the sands of our personal wilderness, we discover once again the GREAT GRACE OF GOD. A gratitude is reborn in our hearts as we learn to lean on Him afresh. He becomes again the Rock of our salvation, the High Tower of refuge, the Shepherd of our souls. We learn again and in a new depth that the Christian life is lived out of gratitude, not grit. Once again the daily manna of His grace becomes deeply refreshing to our souls.

True Grace

When I speak of grace and a vessel of beauty, I am immediately reminded of a young lady I met several years ago. Our first meeting was under somewhat unusual circumstances. At the time we were having a prayer group in our homes, and the constituents of the group were most unusual. They basically came from two differing backgrounds—Marine Corps officers in flight training and conscientious objectors! This was during the latter stages of the Vietnam War, and it was most unusual to find such a group praying together.

I came home late one evening from a difficult day of instructing students, and I walked in on the prayer group in progress. As I sat down and attempted to enter into the flow of the worship that was taking place, I noticed a young couple that I had never seen before. By their dress and hairstyle it was very apparent that they were part of the conscientious objectors we had invited to join us. They were serving as pastoral assistants in a religious community just south of our home.

I noticed the couple because of the great beauty of the young lady. Her beauty was not in the world's sense of feminine beauty, but in the Lord. She literally radiated the grace of God, and appropriately enough her name was Grace.

Over the following months my wife and I became close friends with the couple. Grace's beauty in the Lord was not only apparent in a casual meeting but grew in depth as we came to know her.

During this time in our life the Lord blessed my wife and me with our first child—a little girl. I was now faced with a totally foreign challenge: being a dad to a little girl. I was frankly scared stiff. I was ready for a little boy I could wrestle and play football with. I could help him face the hurdles of being a man of God, but what do you do with a girl?

Honest Before God

Out of the context of that questioning I asked Grace how she had turned out so great. With her characteristic frankness, she said that she had been a brat until she was in her late teens. This was a total shock to me because I knew she had been raised in a Christian home from birth.

After getting over the surprise of her reply, I asked her what turned her around. She began to relate a painful failure in her life—in fact a failure that touched her whole family. The incident would not have appeared crucial to a casual observer. It involved her stealing items from a grocery store. Grace and her father had gone shopping together. During their time at the store, Grace decided it was all right to help herself to some of the merchandise. She was apprehended and brought to the front of the store. In a very messy scene, her father stepped in for her and paid for the stolen items.

As they returned home, her father did not say a word, but Grace could tell that he was deeply grieved. He simply yet firmly told her to go to her room. Grace sat in her room fuming and blaming everyone else for her plight. After a short period of time, she came to the conclusion that she didn't have to obey her father and left the room. Proceeding down a hallway of her home, in an attempt to sneak away from her father, she heard a sound coming from her parents' bedroom.

Pausing at the door, she gently pushed it open. Through the slight crack in the doorway she heard her father praying. He was not complaining about his daughter. He was not moaning over the embarrassment of the failure in his family. He was asking God to search his heart, so that he might understand how he had contributed to the failure. It was not a self-demeaning prayer but an intense cry of personal honesty. He understood that kids imitate their parents and their actions. They occasionally act in a whimsical manner, but a constant pattern of unrighteous acts indicates a parental connection at some point. He was a man who understood the value of failure. He was facing himself and counting on the grace of God.

Grace also noticed that he was being deeply touched by the love of God. It was not a pity party but a praise time. In the midst of great personal pain her father was discovering afresh the grace of God. By this time I was listening to the story with all ears. I was catching an insight into the heart of God. I sensed that I didn't need to be a perfect father to raise a daughter who loved Jesus. I needed instead to be a man who is honest before the Lord, a man who would face the points of his failures with trust in the faithfulness of God.

Faith for the Risk

Raising a family is risky business. That is why so many people in our society avoid the effort. As I listened to Grace I was coming to understand that it may be risky, but that this is just another name for faith. That night I lost some of my fear of fathering as I listened to Grace. If her father could face those kinds of failures and discover afresh the great love of God, so could I. Our ability to be a parent to our children is based on our heavenly Father's faithfulness, not our perfection.

At this point in the story I was sure that Grace would run in and hug her father. That's the way it happens in the movies. She instead quietly closed the door and proceeded down the hall, still determined to get out of the house. But about halfway out of the house it hit her: Her father really loved her and was deeply concerned for her. He wasn't just trying to look good. He truly cared for her no matter what it cost him. At that instant Grace became convinced of the grace of God. She fell to her knees and broke before the Lord. All the bitterness and hatred she had been carefully collecting within her began to crumble away. In the light of honestly facing her failure, she recognized what was happening as she constantly blamed other people. Grace truly started to be Grace that day. She turned to the embrace of Christ's love and chose to be all that she could be in Him.

A part of me was healed that day as I listened to Grace's story. I had come from a family life with six stepfathers. I was even adopted. How could I ever raise a child out of my crippled background?

That day I began to see that it would be by the grace of God. Yes, we will have failures. Yes, sometimes we don't know the first thing about loving a child the way they need to be loved. Yes, we tend to respond in family conflicts out of the wounded patterns of our past. Yet it all doesn't matter because we have a heavenly Father who knows exactly what they need. Our responsibility is to deal openly and honestly with our failures before Him, and He will turn them into foundations of righteousness in our homes.

Failing into the Grace of God

Many years have come and gone since that night. I have failed frequently as a parent, but through it all the Lord has been more than faithful to correct me and equip me to love my children. In the process I have learned more about the character of God from them than I ever have from any theology book.

There is a delicious dialogue that takes place in the clean air of honesty before God. We hear His voice through the mouths of babes. We also grow in our ability to receive from our mate. When failure loses its sting and we begin to see its hidden value, communication between husband and wife can take place in depth. We no longer have to be right all the time. We can listen and not have to defend.

You may find yourself, even today, crying out to God to be set free from your fear of failure in certain areas. It seems that just as you get one area handled, you discover another growth point in your life where you need to face the issue. Yet you have begun to catch on to the fact that it is a lifelong process, a daily process of coming into greater and greater freedom in Christ.

Life is a pilgrimage, and it is normally covered one step at a time. Frequently the steps feel like a fall, but in the timing of God He turns our apparent failures into foundations of growth. If we let Him, He turns even our mistakes into miracles.

FOOTNOTES

1. Otto Freidrich, *Going Crazy* (New York: Simon & Schuster, 1975).
2. Leo Srole, et al, *Mental Health in the Metropolis: The Midtown Manhattan Study*, 2 vols. (New York: McGraw-Hill, 1962).
3. C.E. Izard, *Patterns of Emotions* (New York: Academic Press, 1972).
4. S. Schacter, *Emotion, Obesity & Crime* (New York: Academic Press, 1971).
5. David Stoop, *Self Talk* (Old Tappan, NJ: Revell, 1982).
6. Colin Brown, ed., *Dictionary of New Testament Theology*, vol. 2 (Grand Rapids: Zondervan, 1971), p. 619ff.
7. John Sinclair, "The Hardware of the Brain," in *Psychology Today*, December 1983, pp. 8-12.
8. Wilder Penfield, *The Mystery of the Mind* (Princeton: Princeton University Press, 1975), p. 53.
9. Ibid., p. 108.
10. Charles Swindoll, *Three Steps Forward, Two Steps Back* (Nashville: Thomas Nelson, 1980), p. 74.
11. J. Warren, "Work Out Your Own Salvation," in *Evangelical Quarterly*, vol. 16, 1944, p. 128.
12. W.F. Arndt and F.W. Gingrich, *A Greek-English Lexicon of the New Testament* (Chicago: University of Chicago Press, 1973), p. 114.
13. Kyle Yates, "Hosea," in *New American Standard Bible: Study Edition* (Holomon Co., 1976), p. 877.